Powerful PowerPoint
for Educators

Using Visual Basic for Applications to Make PowerPoint Interactive

David M. Marcovitz

LIBRARIES
UNLIMITED
A Member of the Greenwood Publishing Group

Westport, Connecticut • London

Library of Congress Cataloging-in-Publication Data

Marcovitz, David M.
   Powerful PowerPoint for educators : using Visual Basic for applications to make
PowerPoint interactive / by David M. Marcovitz
      p. cm.
   ISBN: 1–59158–095–1 (alk. paper)
   1. Computer graphics. 2. Microsoft PowerPoint (Computer file) 3. Business
presentations—Graphic methods—Computer programs. 4. Microsoft Visual Basic for
applications. I. Title.
   T385.M36345 2004
   006.6'8682—dc22   2003067183

British Library Cataloguing in Publication Data is available.

Library of Congress Catalog Card Number: 2003067183
ISBN: 1–59158–095–1

First published in 2004

Libraries Unlimited, 88 Post Road West, Westport, CT 06881
A Member of the Greenwood Publishing Group, Inc.
www.lu.com

Printed in the United States of America

The paper used in this book complies with the
Permanent Paper Standard issued by the National
Information Standards Organization (Z39.48–1984).

10   9   8   7   6   5   4   3   2   1

The author maintains a site of supplemental information, including bibliographical updates and further readings. This site is available through Libraries Unlimited site at
www.lu.com.

For the three ladies in my life:
Emily, Ella, and Ada

Contents

List of Figures

Preface

Most educators have created simple presentations with PowerPoint®. PowerPoint is a fine tool for adding media to a lecture, but it falls flat when creating interactive lessons for students to use while sitting in front of the computer. That is, it falls flat unless you use the built-in scripting features of PowerPoint.

Starting with PowerPoint version 97, every copy of PowerPoint comes with Visual Basic® for Applications (VBA). VBA can be used to add to the functionality of Microsoft Office® applications, including Microsoft PowerPoint. With the advent of PowerPoint 97, teachers can put limited interactivity into their presentations using action settings, hyperlinks, and buttons. These features allow you to

- add buttons to control navigation (start your slide show with a menu, for example, rather than requiring linear navigation, from slide to slide to slide);

- jump to other PowerPoint presentations, other files, or Web pages; and

- create rudimentary multiple-choice tests (clicking on a button with the correct answer takes the student to a slide that says "correct," for example).

While this interactivity is useful, it is also very limited. VBA extends this to nearly unlimited dimensions. With VBA, you can change the content and appearance of slides based on student input, ask for and process typed input, add additional slides, hide and show graphics, and much more.

"Wait!" I hear you cry. VBA is a sophisticated programming language. Can teachers become programmers? Certainly, many teachers can become programmers, but the goal is not to create *programmers* but rather *scripters*. A programmer learns all the subtleties of a computer language in minute detail. A scripter might learn some of the details of the language but, more important, learns a few easily modifiable scripts that can perform important tasks. Scripting is well within the reach of many teachers, and taking advantage of the power of authoring systems like PowerPoint is an important part of the International Society for Technology in Education (2001) standards for programs in technology facilitation:

- Standard III.A.7—Use methods for teaching concepts and skills that support use of web-based and non web-based authoring tools in a school environment.

- Standard III.C.1—Use methods and facilitate strategies for teaching problem solving principles and skills using technology resources.
- Standard V.C.7—Use examples of emerging programming, authoring or problem solving environments that support personal and professional development

Scripting might not be a useful technique when used with a stand-alone programming language, but the real power of using VBA with PowerPoint is not merely that VBA is an accessible scripting language but that it is built into PowerPoint. One of my students created a presentation about Hawaii. It included pictures, videos, recorded voices, and links to Web sites. All of this used traditional PowerPoint technology (no scripting required). On top of that, it added an interactive menu and a quiz with feedback about how well the user did on the quiz. Building all of this from scratch with a programming or authoring tool could be an overwhelming task, but 95 percent of the presentation was done with traditional PowerPoint tools (things most teachers already know how to do or can learn within a couple of hours). When a few scripts are added on top of the traditional PowerPoint tools, the results are rich not only with media but also with interactivity.

Remember, the more you know, the more you can do. With a few scripts, you can add short-answer questions (with feedback about right and wrong answers) and keep score. Add a few more scripts and you can have a menu that keeps track of which sections of your presentation have been visited and only shows the button to take the quiz when all sections have been visited. Add a few more scripts and you can have the user type things that change the slides in the presentation. The possibilities are endless.

The more you know, the more you can do. And you can always add more traditional PowerPoint without knowing any more VBA.

I have been using this material (before writing a book about it) with my students, who are mostly teachers, enrolled in a graduate course in multimedia design for the classroom, for about four years. They have created powerful projects for their students (like the Hawaii project mentioned earlier). In addition, I have been speaking about this at conferences and workshops. The overwhelming reaction I get is, "That's great! I didn't know you could do that."

While this book is not accessible for computer novices, teachers who are beyond the level of computer beginner can use this technology to create powerful material for their students, material that goes beyond a simple page-turner.

For the professional multimedia designer, PowerPoint might not be the right choice. However, expensive and complicated tools are not common in schools. Using PowerPoint as a framework, teachers are able to add as much or as little interactivity as their skills allow and their needs require. Thus, PowerPoint is an appropriate multimedia tool for teachers and a powerful addition to a multimedia design class.

This book can be used as a stand-alone book in a multimedia design class for educators or as a companion for books like Ivers and Barron (2002) or Agnew, Kellerman, and Meyer (1996), which focus on multimedia design and using multimedia projects in classrooms but do not deal with a specific technology for implementing the projects. It also stands by itself without a class. Anyone with basic PowerPoint skills can sit down with this book and begin to create powerful educational material for themselves, their colleagues, their students, or their own children.

Chapter 1 begins the book with some important principles of instructional design, including how to design your own projects and create assignments for your students to design their projects. If this book is used in conjunction with a book about design, the first chapter will provide an overview of what you will find in the design books, but if this book is used by itself, this chapter is very important. Jumping in and creating things is fine when you are playing around, but serious projects require some planning and design work, and Chapter 1 will give you a foundation in that.

Chapter 2 begins to explore some of the traditional interactive multimedia features of PowerPoint. Adding pictures, sounds, buttons, and hyperlinks is not difficult, but many PowerPoint users have never used those features before.

Chapter 3 introduces VBA. You'll understand how VBA fits into the world of object-oriented programming and how that affects you as a scripter. As a scripter, you won't have to understand all of VBA and object-oriented programming, but understanding objects and how to manipulate them will help you understand your scripts.

Chapter 4 begins the heart of the book as you start to learn about scripting with VBA. You'll learn how VBA is connected to PowerPoint and how to write and run your first script. You'll also learn about keeping your scripts private so your students can't look for the answers in your scripts.

Chapters 5 and 6 build your bag of scripting tricks. As a scripter, you will be interested in taking scripts directly from these chapters and applying them to your own purposes.

While each chapter contains examples that you can use right away, Chapter 7 focuses on examples that you will be able to use to create quizzes and tests.

Once you have completed Chapter 7, you will have a large bag of tricks that you can use by copying scripts directly from the book and possibly creating some on your own. Chapter 8 describes some more tricks that you can use, particularly if you are ready to modify some of the ideas in the book for your own purposes. It ends with a powerful example that I use with my daughter as she is learning to read.

Once you have mastered a large bag of tricks, you might need some help correcting your mistakes. Whenever you write scripts, even if you just copy them from the book, you are likely to make a few mistakes. Fixing mistakes is called debugging, and you will learn some of the secrets of debugging in Chapter 9.

By the time you finish Chapter 9, you will be excited to create things yourself, but you might want to share your knowledge with your colleagues and your students. Some of them will share your enthusiasm and borrow your copy of this book (or better yet, buy their own copy) and dive right into powerful PowerPoint. Others won't be ready for the technical challenge. Chapter 10 describes how you can use templates, so your colleagues and students can take full advantage of the power of VBA scripting without knowing any of it. You can use what you learn in Chapter 10 to provide a template for your colleagues or students with the scripting already done for them (by you).

When you have completed the book, you might not be an expert at using VBA to create powerful interactive multimedia projects, but you will have a large bag of tricks that can help you do more with technology to make you a better educator.

Writing this book has been a long process. I began my journey when I attended a presentation at a conference in which the speaker was talking about all the exciting educational things that can be done with PowerPoint. I thought that he was talking about the things this book discusses, but I was wrong. I started exploring, and I found that no one was talking about these things, at least not for educators. As I looked for books to help me, I found many (look in the References section at the end of the book), but none was geared to educators or to using PowerPoint interactively. I wanted to share this with my students, so I started creating my own handouts. As the handouts grew, I began speaking about this at conferences and giving workshops. Everyone was amazed at what PowerPoint could do. By the time the handouts reached seventy pages, I knew it was time to move from handouts to a book.

I would like to thank all the people who helped me along the way, but they are too numerous to mention, so I will mention only a few. I would like to thank all my students over the years in Multimedia Design in the Classroom, particularly the first group, who had to endure the course with a few pages of handouts that were being written during the course, in most cases the night before each class. I also would like to thank Diana Sucich, one of my students who reviewed the manuscript as it was morphing from a seventy-page packet of handouts into a book. Her comments were invaluable. I also would like to thank Luis Bango, a former student who suffered through Multimedia Design in the Classroom while the handouts were not in the best shape and reviewed the final manuscript. I also would like to thank the PowerPoint MVPs in the Microsoft PowerPoint newsgroup. Several PowerPoint experts give their time in that newsgroup to answer questions from beginners and experts alike with beginning PowerPoint questions and complex scripting questions.

Finally, I would like to thank my family. My wife Emily has provided me with unending love and support as I have stayed late in the office to work on the book. My daughter Ella has been a guinea pig for some of my wacky projects, particularly the example at the end of Chapter 9. Both my children, Ella and Ada, have provided me with love and inspiration because I hope that my work will help my children and all children by making the computer a more effective tool for education.

You are about to embark on a great journey. At times you will be elated and at times frustrated. If you persevere, you will have the power to make the computer do what you want it to, so it can be a tool for you and your students' learning. The computer shouldn't be everything in education, but when it is used, it should be used powerfully and effectively.

Multimedia Design

Introduction

Welcome to the world of powerful PowerPoint. This book will help you use PowerPoint in ways you never thought were possible, with the ultimate goal of creating better learning environments for your students. Whatever you do as an educator requires some planning, whether it takes the form of detailed lesson plans or a few notes jotted on the back of a napkin. When creating complex learning environments, planning is very important. This chapter introduces some of the basics of planning and design to help you create better learning environments. You will be introduced to the benefits of multimedia, the design process, benefits of having your students design multimedia, and metaphors and organizations for multimedia projects.

Vocabulary

- Decide
- Design
- Develop
- Evaluate
- Formative evaluation
- Metaphor
- Organization
- Storyboard
- Summative evaluation

What Is Multimedia?

Multimedia is a term that has been around for a long time. Before computers, it referred to a combination of slides (from a slide projector) and sounds (usually music from a tape player). It has been around for so long because people have recognized that we can be engaged through multiple senses. Some people are primarily visual learners, auditory learners, or kinesthetic learners, but most of us are a combination of all three. Using different senses increases attention, motivation, and, in many cases, learning. "The power of multimedia and hypermedia presentation software comes with changes in the ways teachers and learners have access to and demonstrate their understanding of knowledge, moving from a single dominant presentation and demonstration style (verbal/linguistic, linear/sequential) to an integrated, multisensory learning and demonstration 'microworld' (Papert, 1992), where learners have more freedom of choice in the mode of learning and the order in which learning takes place" (Male, 2003, p. 6). As this quote suggests, multimedia involves multiple senses and a degree of learner control and choice.

Robinette suggests, "Multimedia is about combining sights, sounds, and interactive elements to create an experience unlike that which comes from simply reading text or idly viewing a video" (1995, p. 10). Goldberg says, "Multimedia, as I use it to define the cool new medium that I've been going on about, is the combination of audio/visual media elements with interactivity. . . . A typical multimedia title might include any combination of text, pictures, computer graphics, animation, audio, and video" (1996, p. 14).

Multimedia is about including a variety of media with interactivity. Typical presentations (using PowerPoint or other presentation tools) emphasize the media and not the interactivity. When enhancing a lecture to present to an audience, interactivity is not always important. However, when creating projects that your students can control, picking and choosing where to go within the project, well-designed interactivity is very important.

Interactive multimedia helps students learn by increasing motivation, by giving them control over their learning, and by reaching them through different senses. As you design multimedia presentations for your students, you decide what media are most appropriate. Sometimes a picture is worth a thousand words; sometimes a few words are worth a thousand pictures; and sometimes, in the case of a struggling reader, for example, spoken words are more important than everything else. A few bells and whistles, used sparingly and appropriately, can increase motivation and hold your students' attention, but a carefully designed project with appropriate media elements can be a powerful experience for the learner. The key is to design your projects well.

The Design Process

While playing around on the computer is useful to help you understand the technology and brainstorm ideas for your project, the best projects come from careful planning. When you first start a project, you might think that you are saving time by jumping right in and creating the project, but you are not. Agnew, Kellerman, and Meyer (1996) outline a twelve-step process for designing and developing a multimedia project:

1. Understand the scope of the project/assignment.
2. Brainstorm and do research.
3. Select pieces of information to include in the project.
4. Discuss several overall organizations.
5. Select an organization.
6. Decide on a metaphor for visualizing the body of information.
7. Decide on one or more media to represent each piece of information.
8. Prepare scripts and storyboards as required.
9. Fill in the organization with media.
10. Provide links among pieces of information.
11. Test the result with typical members of the project's intended audience.
12. Revise the project.

Ivers and Barron (2002) propose the DDD-E model: decide, design, develop, evaluate. Other instructional design models are more complex, but these two models capture the important aspects of instructional design.

Don't worry about following a specific step-by-step process. Most of the steps overlap, and some steps, such as evaluation, are continuous and take place at every stage of the process. That doesn't mean you should jump right to developing your project before deciding and designing—there is a general flow from step to step—but creating a project involves continuous evaluation and may involve rethinking and redesigning parts of the project as the project begins to take shape.

Before beginning, you must *decide* what you want to do and what you want your students to get out of the project. This includes understanding the scope of the project and brainstorming ideas for the project. Starting with a clear idea of what you want the project to cover is very useful. If you have certain objectives (from your curriculum or not), those objectives will help you determine what your project should cover. Try to limit the scope of the project, keeping in mind the limits of your students' attention span. Create a project that is small or build in features that allow students to quit in the middle and come back to explore other parts of the project.

Don't be afraid to brainstorm ideas. That means that you can come up with ideas for what you want to include that will be rejected later. This is part of the power of planning. If you create half your project first, you have either locked yourself into something that might not be what you want, or you have wasted a great deal of time creating something that you will throw away. By playing with ideas in the early stages of the design process, you can narrow down what you want to do without throwing away large amounts of work.

While you are *deciding* what the project should include, research your subject. Be sure you understand the subject so you can create something that will help others learn it. As you research, you should *decide* what information you want to include and begin to collect the media you will use to represent that information.

As you *decide*, keep in mind that your decisions are not set in stone. You should complete the *decide* phase having a good idea of what you want to do, but you should understand that the details can and will change as you move forward with your project.

Once you have an idea about what your project will entail, you should begin to *design* it. You will *design* the organization and metaphor for the project (more about this in the next sections), you will create a storyboard for the project to help you understand the flow and interaction of the project, and you will *design* the individual slides, figuring out what content and media go on each slide. Now your project is taking shape, and you should have a fairly clear picture of what the final project will look like. But again, this is not set in stone. The details can and will change, but they should change within the overall framework you have *designed*.

Next, it is time to *develop* your project. This involves filling in the pieces: creating or acquiring any media elements you need, creating your slides, placing your media elements and buttons on your slides, and linking it all together. This is much easier when you know what you want to do, having *decided* on the project and having *designed* the project first. The hardest part will be writing your scripts to make the project do what you want it to do, and you will learn how to do that beginning in Chapter 3.

The final phase is not really the final phase: *evaluate*. *Evaluation* is a continuous and ongoing process. You will conduct formative *evaluation*, in which you check your work to make sure that everything seems to be doing what you want, and you enlist others to check your work as well. This can happen at many different points in the process, and it can be done by many different people, including: you, your colleagues, your students, and other members of the intended audience for the project. This formative *evaluation* will provide you with feedback to improve the project.

You also will conduct summative *evaluation* when the project is complete. As with any lesson, you want to think about specific ways you will know how well the project worked with your students. This can be used to decide whether or not you want to use the project again, and it can provide feedback for things you might want to change about the project for next time.

Project Organization

As part of the design process, you must think about how your project will be organized. Chapter 2 describes how to create hyperlinks in PowerPoint, and Chapter 6 describes how to use VBA to move from any slide to any other. However, just because you can make links from any slide to any other doesn't mean that you want to. A project with a clear organization will help your students find their way around the project.

There are several ways to organize a project. The simplest organization is linear, in which the user goes from one slide to the next to the next to the next (see Figure 1.1). This works very well for projects in which knowledge is being built from prerequisite knowledge or in which specific steps are followed in a specific order.

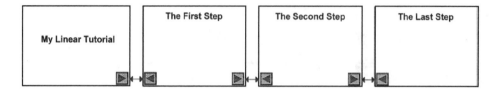

Figure 1.1. Linear Organization

However, many projects don't require a linear organization and would benefit from some other organization. Fortunately, hypermedia allows us to link any slide to any slide that we want. We could follow a menu organization (see Figure 1.2, page 6). This organization allows the user to study the topics in whatever order he or she wants and even allows the user to skip topics.

Some topics lend themselves better to a hierarchical menu structure in which each subtopic has its own menu. Other projects might do better with a completely hyperlinked organization in which any slide can lead to any other slide.

The organization you choose should match the objectives of the project. If it is not appropriate for students to skip sections, don't allow it. You provide links where you want your students to go (and in Chapter 2, you'll learn about Kiosk mode so you can make sure they only go where you want).

There are many potential structural organizations, but it is helpful to pick something that will allow the user to navigate easily through your information. If the structure is not easy to navigate, when a user goes through your presentation, it is easy to get lost in hyperspace.

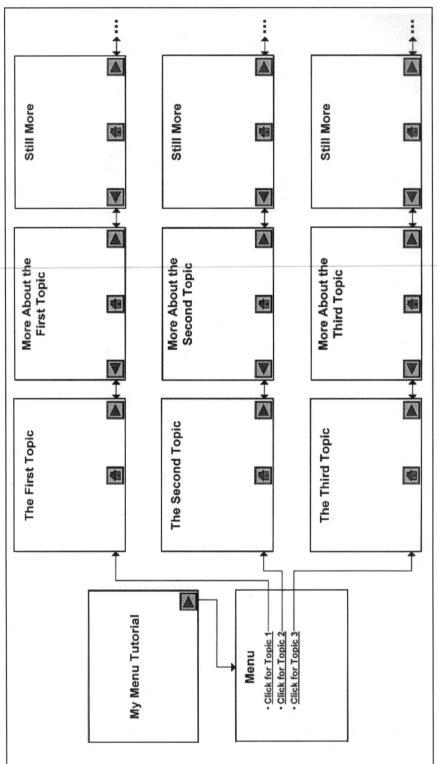

Figure 1.2. Menu Organization

Metaphors

A metaphor is the way the user will think about the project. For example, a geography project might choose a map metaphor where users click on certain locations on a map to visit the location. You might choose a book metaphor, starting with a cover and a table of contents and referring to each slide as a page (complete with page numbers and graphics that make the slides look like pages). Metaphors can be complex or simple, with more complex metaphors providing somewhat of an illusion that the user is actually in the metaphor. For example, a travel metaphor might include animations of planes taking off and landing to give the illusion that the user is actually going someplace.

Metaphors can be particularly helpful when you are not creating a project but are assigning your students to create a project. This helps students to "unleash their creativity by finding new metaphors for information. Metaphors stimulate visualizations" (Agnew, Kellerman, and Meyer, 1996, p. 121). Metaphors are a powerful tool to help users navigate a project and to help designers think creatively about a project.

Storyboards and Flowcharts

Once you have chosen an organization and a metaphor for your project, you need to figure out how the entire project will work. The more complex the project, the more this step is needed. At a minimum, you should sketch in advance your entire project, not necessarily with all the details, but with enough details so you can see how the project holds together. Indicate how each slide will be linked to any other slides and the kinds of (if not the exact) information that will be on each slide.

Although you can do this with a computer drawing program, a small screen size is limiting. You might want to map out your project on a large poster board or a giant piece of newsprint. Index cards can represent each slide in your project. You can use formal flowcharting symbols (see, for example, Ivers and Barron, 2002, pp. 64–65), or you can use a less formal system, but you must understand and map out the project.

If you are not creating the project yourself but assigning it to your students, this step becomes even more important. Your students are unlikely to do any planning unless you specifically require it and require them to hand in their designs. When they don't plan, the quality of their work will suffer, and the time it takes for them to complete their work will increase.

As you design the flow of your project, you also need to map out what will happen on each slide. You might use your giant flowchart to fill in the details, or you might use the cards on your flowchart as placeholders and have a separate drawing of each slide. As you plan the flow of your project and what information goes on each slide, you will be able to broaden and narrow your view of the project, alternately seeing an overview of the project and focusing on the details.

This will help you adjust your design as you need to. It is much easier to move a card or add a card or delete a card than it is to take a half-finished project, including VBA scripts, and move everything around, rewriting the scripts to match the redesign.

This does not mean that your design is fixed once you start developing your project. But with a good idea of how the project works and most of the details in place, you will find it easier to create the project and make changes as needed.

Designing Assignments for Your Students

As powerful as it is to create multimedia projects for your students, it is more powerful to have them create their own multimedia projects. While the project you create can increase motivation and tap into different learning styles, having students create their own projects is an outstanding vehicle for creating a student-centered and constructivist learning environment, for taking a multidisciplinary approach to education, and for helping students understand information and media.

Projects you assign can be simple or complex, involving a few different types of media or several, using a simple design structure that you assign or a complex structure and metaphor that your students choose. As you continue through this book, you will learn advanced techniques for making PowerPoint do what you want it to do. You might share these techniques with your students, or you might let them create less complex projects. Another alternative is to create templates for your students in which you create the basic structure of the project, using simple or advanced PowerPoint techniques, and have your students fill in the template with content and media. Templates are discussed in Chapter 10.

Student projects need to follow a similar design process to any other multimedia projects. However, as a teacher, you must decide (1) how much you want to provide for your students and (2) how much help you want to give your students at each step.

First, you must create an assignment in a way that students can understand. Agnew, Kellerman, and Meyer (1996, pp. 120–121) outline four keys to help students create a well-organized multimedia project:

1.   "[A]rticulate a well-thought-out assignment."

2.   "[D]emonstrate excellent examples of projects that others have created."

3.   "[E]ncourage students to unleash their creativity by finding new metaphors for information."

4.   Help "students execute an effective process."

As an educator, you probably are comfortable creating assignments for your students. However, multimedia projects can be larger and more complex than ordinary assignments. Being clear abut your purpose and expectations can help students understand what they are supposed to do and help them meet and exceed your expectations. Be sure to match the project you assign to your curricular goals and the technical skills of your students. If you plan to have students create several multimedia projects, you can make the first project simple to help them understand the technology. As their technology skills grow, the projects can be more complex.

Many students need concrete examples. The more multimedia you do (for yourself or your students), the more examples you will have to show students.

You also want to encourage creative thinking, including brainstorming ideas for metaphors. A metaphor helps a user navigate through a project by giving the user something from the real world to relate to what the controls (such as buttons and hypertext links) do. Metaphors can be closely related to the project or can be an unrelated navigation and visualization tools. You can provide your students with a metaphor (this might be appropriate for early projects), you can brainstorm different metaphors for different projects as a class, you can brainstorm with groups about metaphors for a specific project, or you can have groups brainstorm on their own.

Finally, you will want to help your students with the design process. Students might need help with all the design steps. You can give your students help with all of the following:

- **The Idea**—A good assignment will have a clear set of objectives, but it might allow students a great deal of latitude in picking a topic. You might need to work with students to help them generate ideas for their topic.

- **The Research**—Since one purpose of multimedia projects is to enhance learning in curricular areas, you will have to decide how much of the research you will provide for the students. You could provide all the information that will be used in the project. You could provide specific resources for students. You could help students find materials (in the library or on the Internet, for example). You could brainstorm ideas with students about where they might find the information they need.

- **Selecting Information**—Many students have trouble finding enough information, and many have trouble selecting the information to include. You might need to help students narrow down the appropriate information to include; they might not be able to include everything they find.

- **The Organization and the Metaphor**—You might pick an organization and a metaphor for your students or help them find an appropriate organization and metaphor.

- **The Media**—Students might need help selecting and preparing the media representations of their information. You might help them decide what medium to use for each kind of information, and you might help them with the technical process of creating or finding the media representations. In the extreme case, you might give them prepared media to use in their projects.

- **Templates**—You might provide a template for your students. This can provide a metaphor, organization, and/or types of media.

In any of the above cases, you need to decide what is appropriate for your students. Sometimes the best policy is to leave the students alone. At other times, you will need to coach them throughout the entire project. At a minimum, your students will need to check in with you on a regular basis, showing you the design at various phases. It is often a good idea to set deadlines for various parts of the project, requiring students to turn in something to you at each of the twelve steps of the design process (see "The Design Process" above) or at one or more points along the way.

Multimedia projects are often an excellent vehicle for group projects. But groups can be difficult. You may decide whether you want to group students by ability levels, interests, skills, or their own choice. Once you have groups, generally of between two and five students, you need to help students work out the roles they will play in the group. Some projects have natural roles that students can play, dividing the project either by subject matter or technical specialty (gathering information, video production, VBA scripting, etc.). Learning to work with a group can be an important objective of the project, but group dynamics can be difficult, and you will have to monitor how well members of the groups are working together.

Be careful about selecting the requirements for your project. Make sure that they are suitable for your goals. Remember that part of the idea of learning multimedia is to see that great artwork or sounds do not necessarily mean great information. Make sure that, if your goal is to have worthwhile information, students are aware that that is important.

Finally, try to save time for reflection. A great deal of the learning (for you and your students) can come from looking back at the projects and seeing what went right and what went wrong and what was learned.

Conclusion

This chapter has given you a brief introduction to multimedia, including what it is and what its benefits are, and has introduced you to the design process. If you plan carefully, you will save yourself time and limit frustration, and you will create better projects. Finally, the chapter introduced some ideas for having your students be multimedia designers. This chapter was an introduction to, rather than complete coverage of, the design process. You might want to check out Ivers and Barron (2002) or Agnew, Kellerman, and Meyer (1996), which provide more details about the design process and using multimedia with students.

Now that you have a basic understanding of the design process, you are ready to apply it to PowerPoint. The next chapter introduces some of the interactive and multimedia features of PowerPoint and prepares you to conquer the advanced scripting features of PowerPoint in later chapters.

Traditional Multimedia Features of PowerPoint

Introduction

Some people, even long-time PowerPoint users, are not aware of many of the multimedia and interactive features of PowerPoint. Most of this book describes how you can use scripting features of PowerPoint to make presentations interactive. This chapter briefly describes some of the multimedia and interactive features that do not require scripting. You will learn about media elements, such as pictures and sounds, and you will learn about interactive elements such as hyperlinks and action buttons. In addition, you will learn about the important differences in Slide Show View and Edit View when editing your slides. Finally, you will learn about Kiosk mode and saving your project as a PowerPoint Show to control how your students navigate through your presentation.

Vocabulary

- Action buttons
- Clip art
- Copyright
- Edit View
- Embedded
- Fair use
- Hyperlinks
- Hypertext
- Kiosk mode
- Linked
- PowerPoint Show (.pps)
- Slide Show View

Before You Begin

This book assumes that you know the basics of PowerPoint. If you don't, you should spend a couple of hours playing with PowerPoint and/or buy an introductory book about PowerPoint. Try to get one that is specific to the version of PowerPoint that you own. While most features are identical from version to version, there are a few subtle differences in each version.

Before you begin, you should check a few of PowerPoint's settings. Start PowerPoint, and choose "Options" from the Tools menu if you are using a Windows computer, choose "Preferences" from the Edit menu if you are using a Macintosh with OS 9 or earlier, and choose "Preferences" from the PowerPoint menu if you are using a Macintosh with OS X. Regardless of which version you are using, you will have several tabs at the top of the dialog box. These tabs include View, General, Edit, and Save. The remaining tabs will vary by which version you have.

Click on the Save tab. The first item is a check box for "Allow fast saves" (see Figure 2.1). If this box is checked, click on it to remove the check mark. If you allow fast saves, PowerPoint will spend less time saving your work, but it will create larger files and files that are more prone to problems. While you are unlikely to ever find that PowerPoint has corrupted your project, you are less likely to have problems if you uncheck "Allow fast saves."

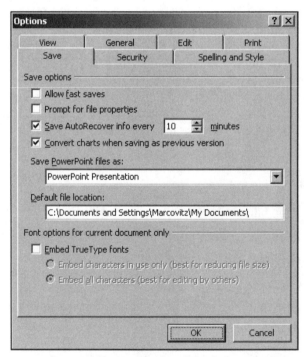

Figure 2.1. No Check Next to "Allow fast saves"

Next, click on the Edit tab. Find the "Undo" section. Change the setting for "Maximum number of undos" to 10. In many applications, when you make a mistake, if you don't do anything else, you can fix it by choosing "Undo" from the Edit menu. In PowerPoint, you can fix not only the last mistake but several mistakes before that. This setting tells PowerPoint how many things it has to remember so you can undo them. In theory, you might want to have as many as possible, but several PowerPoint experts have noticed that the higher this number is the more likely you are to have problems with PowerPoint. Setting it to 10 gives you enough ability to correct your mistakes while minimizing the likelihood that you will have a problem.

Another setting you might want to change can be found under the General tab. You might want to change the setting for "Link sounds with file size greater than." This setting is discussed later in this chapter.

Once you have changed the settings to not allow fast saves and to limit the number of undos, click OK to save the settings.

Next, choose "Customize" from the Tools menu. Click on the Toolbars tab and make sure there is a check next to "Drawing." The "Drawing" toolbar will be very useful for drawing your own shapes and modifying the appearance of shapes that are drawn for you.

Finally, before you start working on a PowerPoint project, create a folder on your disk for your project and save your presentation to that folder. This will be important when you start including hyperlinks and multimedia objects in your presentation. Most elements of your presentation will be embedded in your presentation. That is, they will be part of the PowerPoint file. Other elements will be stored in other files, and your presentation will link to those other files. If you save your presentation first and you save any linked files to the same place you save your presentation (that is, the same folder on the same disk), your links will continue to work when you move the presentation (along with all the linked files) to another place, such as another folder, another disk, or another computer. If you don't save your files first, the links are likely to stop working.

Inserting Pictures

You can insert pictures into a PowerPoint presentation in several different ways, including by inserting from the clip art library, by inserting from an existing file, and by copying and pasting from another place, including the World Wide Web. In addition, if you are artistically inclined, you can use the drawing tools to draw your own pictures. Generally pictures are embedded in your PowerPoint presentation. That is, once you insert them, they become part of the presentation, regardless of what happens to the original picture.

PowerPoint recognizes many different types of picture files, including most of the common ones you are likely to encounter, such as Graphic Interchange Format (.gif), Joint Photographic Experts Group (.jpg), Tag Image File Format (.tif or .tiff), and Bitmap (.bmp). If you try to insert a picture into your presentation and PowerPoint gives you an error or asks you how to convert it, you will need to find a program (such as GraphicConverter™ or Adobe Photoshop™) that can read that file type and create files of one of the types that PowerPoint can read.

To insert a picture from a file, choose "Picture" from the Insert menu and choose "From File . . ." from the flyout menu (see Figure 2.2).

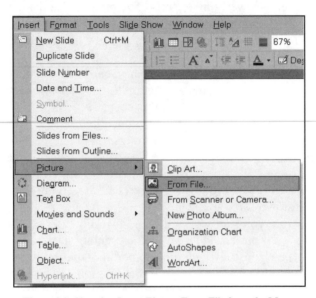

Figure 2.2. Choosing Insert Picture From File from the Menu

Although the dialog box you see will vary slightly depending upon which version of PowerPoint you are using, it should look similar to the dialog box you see whenever you try to open a file on your computer. From this point, locate the file with the picture you want to insert and click on the "Insert" button.

While inserting a picture from a file has remained fairly consistent from version to version of PowerPoint, inserting clip art has changed quite a bit. You start by choosing "Clip Art . . . " from the flyout menu instead of "From File . . . " (see Figure 2.2). In PowerPoint 2002, you can search for clip art using the dialog shown in Figure 2.3, use the Clip Organizer, or search Microsoft's fairly extensive collection of clip art on the Web. From Microsoft's Web collection, you can download clip art into your own collection so you can use it later without going to the Web.

Figure 2.3. Insert Clip Art in PowerPoint 2002

Another way to add graphics to your presentation is to copy and paste. Generally, if you can see it on your computer you can copy it into your presentation. However, you must be careful; although you might be able to copy a picture into your presentation, you might not have the right to copy it into your presentation. Be sure to follow copyright law and guidelines, noting that just because you don't see a copyright symbol © does not mean that the picture or Web page is not copyrighted. While the fair use aspects of copyright law give you a great deal of freedom to use copyrighted material for educational purposes, many restrictions apply as to what you can use, how much you can use, and for how long you can use it. Your best bet is to use material you have created yourself, material that is in the public domain (see for example, http://www.pics4learning.com/), or material for which you have obtained permission to use. But if you must use copyrighted material without permission, you should pay close attention to the Fair Use Guidelines for Educational Multimedia (see http://www.utsystem.edu/ogc/ intellectualproperty/ccmcguid.htm). While these guidelines are not the law, they are a good guide for your fair-use rights to use copyrighted material.

If you are on the Web and you see a picture that you want to use and you have the right to use it because of fair use, because the picture is in the public domain, or because you have permission to use it, you can generally copy it into your PowerPoint presentation. If you are on a Macintosh, point your mouse to the picture you want to copy and hold the mouse button down until you see a menu that pops up. If you are on a Windows computer, point your mouse to the picture and right click (that is, click the right mouse button; see Figure 2.4).

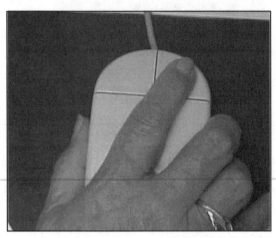

Figure 2.4. Right Click the Mouse

The flyout menu that you see should look something like the menu in Figure 2.5. It will vary from browser to browser, but you should see "Copy" as one of your choices. Choose "Copy" (by clicking or left clicking on the choice in the menu). Now, when you switch back to your PowerPoint presentation, you can choose "Paste" from the Edit menu to put the picture in your presentation.

Once a picture is in PowerPoint, it is an object, and you can move it around, resize it, or even assign it actions. Pictures are always embedded in the presentation, so you don't need the original picture file to see the picture within PowerPoint.

Sounds

PowerPoint presentations can include sounds in a wide range of formats. Like pictures, the sounds can be inserted from clip art or from a file. Sounds can also refer to a CD track or be recorded, assuming you have a microphone connected to your computer. You can make the appropriate selection by choosing "Movies and Sounds" from the Insert menu.

If you choose to use a CD track for your sound, then the CD must be in the computer when you are inserting the sound and whenever you are running the presentation. This works well if you are presenting something to an audience, but it works poorly if you are putting the presentation on several computers for your students. A better alternative might be to import the CD track into your computer, but you must be careful about copyright guidelines, which limit the amount of a song you may use to 10 percent of the song or thirty seconds, whichever is less.

Figure 2.5. Flyout Menu to Copy a Picture from a Browser

Recording your own sounds is a good option because, in an educational setting, much of the sound that is valuable is text that is read. If you teach students who are still learning to read or students with special needs, providing a button to have text read can be very useful. If you teach proficient readers, allowing new or difficult vocabulary to be read can be very helpful. When you choose "Record Sound" from the "Movies and Sounds" flyout menu of the Insert menu, you will get a dialog box like the one in Figure 2.6. (Note that this dialog box will look a little different depending upon which version of PowerPoint you are using.) Be sure that you give your sound a specific name so all your sounds are not named "Recorded Sound." Click on the circle to begin recording your sound and click on the square to stop recording. Click on the triangle to listen to the sound.

The biggest problem with sounds is inserting them into your presentation on one computer only to find that they don't play on another computer. This usually has to do with whether the sounds are linked or embedded.

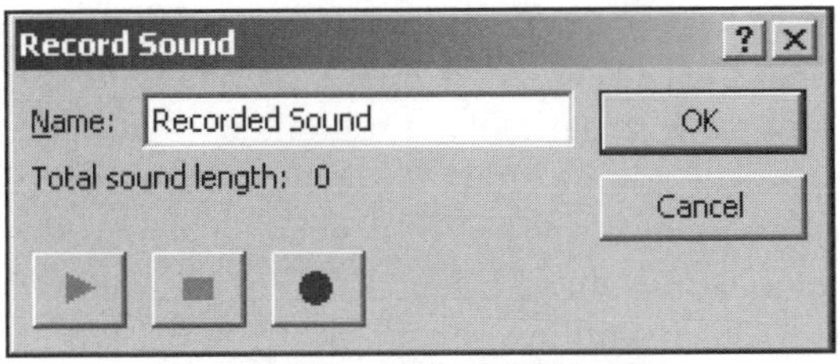

Figure 2.6. Record Sound Dialog Box

Linking and Embedding Sounds

When you include some elements in PowerPoint, they are embedded in your PowerPoint presentation. That means that the element becomes part of the PowerPoint file. Other elements are inserted as links to other files. Pictures are generally embedded in the presentation. Movies are links to other files. This means that if you insert a picture into a PowerPoint presentation, you no longer need the original picture. The PowerPoint presentation has the picture inside it, so you can move the presentation to another disk or delete the original picture, and the presentation will still show the picture. If you insert a movie into a PowerPoint presentation, the movie is not part of the PowerPoint file. The PowerPoint presentation contains a pointer to the file. If you move the PowerPoint presentation to another disk or delete the original movie, your presentation will no longer play the movie.

Sometimes sounds are embedded, and sometimes they are linked. Two things affect whether they are embedded or linked: the type of sound and the size of the sound. Sounds of type Audio Format (.au), Audio Interchange File Format (.aif or .aiff), and Musical Instrument Digital Interface (.midi or .mid) are always linked. Sounds of type Waveform Audio (.wav) can be linked or embedded depending on the size of the sound. Waveform Audio sounds that are greater than the size of the "Link sounds with file size greater than" setting will be linked. Waveform Audio sounds that are smaller than that setting are embedded. You can change this setting by going to the "General" tab of your "Preferences" or "Options" (the place you made many of the changes to settings in the "Before You Begin" section of this chapter). Look for the number next to "Link sounds with file size greater than." This number is in kilobytes and usually starts at 100. Most clip sounds (such as boings and beeps and applause) are far less than 100kB, but longer sounds can be larger. I generally set this setting to 999kB to ensure that most of the sounds I use will be embedded.

In the "Before You Begin" section of this chapter, I suggested that you create a folder for your PowerPoint project and save your presentation there before you do anything. This is to prevent problems with linked files. It is fine to have linked files in your PowerPoint presentation, whether they are sounds or movies or other files. The key is to make sure that the links work when you move your presentation to another disk or another computer. If you have saved your PowerPoint presentation to a folder, and you have saved any linked files to that same folder before linking to those files, your presentation should be portable as long as you move all the files together (i.e., move the whole folder).

Linked files become a particular problem with sounds or movies taken from the Clip Organizer. On different computers with different operating systems (even different versions of Windows), even the standard clip sounds can be located in different locations. In addition, different computers have different clip sounds loaded on them. If you insert a sound from the Clip Organizer and the sound is linked, there is a good chance that the sound will not play on other computers. To alleviate this, you should find out where the sound is located on your computer and copy the sound you intend to use into your folder with the presentation. On my Windows computer, many of the standard clip sounds can be found in the folder: "C:\Program Files\Microsoft Office\media\CntCD1\Sounds," but that is unlikely to be where they are on your computer. On my Macintosh, the standard clip sounds can be found in "Macintosh HD:Applications:Microsoft Office X:Office:Sounds."

Are My Sounds Linked or Embedded?

If you have inserted a sound and it is embedded, you do not need to worry about where the sound file is. If it is linked, you do need to worry about it. While knowing the size of the sound, the size of your setting for "Link sounds with file size greater than," and the type of sound will help you predict whether the sound will be linked or embedded, you will want to check to be sure.

Once you have inserted a sound, click on the sound icon and choose "Sound Object" from the Edit menu. At the bottom of the dialog box, you will see "File:" and either "[Contained in presentation]" or a path to the file. The former indicates an embedded file, and the latter indicates a linked file. While the path to the file might help you locate the file (so you can copy it to your project folder), the dialog box is generally too small to show the entire path.

Hypertext Links

Before version 97, PowerPoint was simply a tool to present material. Presenters would stand up in front of an audience and go through slide after slide. PowerPoint's advantage was that media (text, graphics, sounds, videos, etc.) could be incorporated into the presentation to add bells and whistles and to present information in a variety of formats. PowerPoint 97 changed all that. OK, PowerPoint 97 changed very little of that because most people still use PowerPoint for linear presentations. However, PowerPoint 97 allows you to use it in different ways.

One tool that was added to PowerPoint was hyperlinks. Hyperlinks allow you to create presentations that are nonlinear. With the popularity of the World Wide Web, everyone is used to clicking on text to jump somewhere, and PowerPoint gives you that capability. You can create hypertext links to other places in your presentation, to Web pages, and to other files.

Linking Within Your Presentation

Being able to link to other places in your file makes PowerPoint a more powerful presentation tool, but it also gives you the power to create projects that users navigate themselves. Presentations no longer have to go from one slide to

the next to the next to the next. You can make them go anywhere. If you are giving a presentation, you might want to link to slides with the answers to questions
you anticipate being asked. If you are creating something for your students, you
might use a menu structure in which students choose a topic from a menu and
when finished with that topic, jump back to the menu.

To link to another place within your PowerPoint presentation, create a few
slides first, perhaps creating a menu slide that will link to the other slides. Highlight the text you want to link and choose "Hyperlink" from the Insert menu. Be
sure to highlight the text; if you don't, PowerPoint will make a single word the
link. See Figure 2.7.

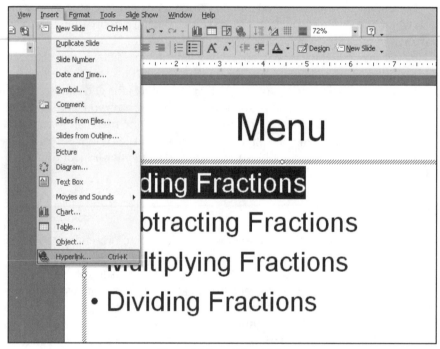

Figure 2.7. Insert Hyperlink

The exact format of the dialog box that you see will vary based on which
version of PowerPoint you use, but it should look very similar to Figure 2.8 or
Figure 2.9.

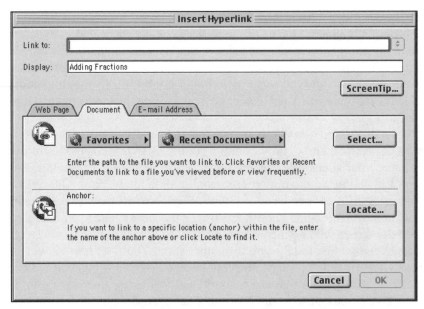

Figure 2.8. Insert Hyperlink Dialog in PowerPoint 2001

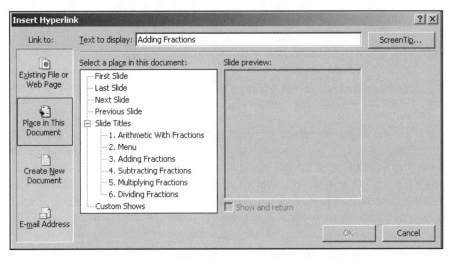

Figure 2.9. Insert Hyperlink Dialog in PowerPoint 2002

In some versions, you will see tabs for "Web Page," "Document," and "E-mail Address" (see Figure 2.8). In other versions, you will see tabs for "Existing File or Web Page," "Place in This Document," "Create New Document," and "E-mail Address" (see Figure 2.9). To link your text to another slide, choose "Document" or "Place in This Document." If your screen looks like Figure 2.8, click on the "Locate . . . " button in the "Anchor" section of the dialog box. Now your screen should look like part of Figure 2.9 with choices to link to "First

Slide," "Last Slide," "Next Slide," "Previous Slide," "Slide Titles," and "Custom Shows." If you don't have any choices for slides under "Slide Titles," click on the triangle or plus sign next to "Slide Titles" and the names of all your slides should appear. This is where you can choose a particular slide to link to. Click on the slide title to which you want to link and click OK. The highlighted text should become underlined and change color (based on the colors in the template you are using).

Some of you tried to click on your text, and it didn't take you anywhere. That's OK. As you know, PowerPoint has different views or modes in which you can see your slides. We can edit our slides in Edit View (sometimes called Normal View), but we run our presentation in Slide Show View. Our links will only work in Slide Show View. Choose "View Show" from the Slide Show menu to take you into Slide Show View (that's the view where you only see your slide on the screen with no menus or toolbars). Now you should be able to click on your hypertext link to take you to another slide. You'll notice that when you point to a hypertext link (or any element of PowerPoint on which you can click), your cursor changes from an arrow to a hand. Watch for that change in Slide Show View so you can see what is clickable and what is not.

Once you have linked one part of a menu, it is easy to follow the same steps to link the rest of the items in the menu: Highlight the text you want linked, choose "Hyperlink . . . " from the Insert menu, choose "Document" or "Place in This Document," click on the plus sign or triangle if necessary to see the titles of your slides, click the appropriate slide title, and click OK.

Linking Outside Your Presentation: Web Pages and Other Documents

While linking within your presentation allows your presentation to be interactive, linking outside your presentation allows the interactivity to extend beyond PowerPoint and allows your PowerPoint document to serve as a springboard to other resources. During a lecture, you can jump to a relevant Web site via a link in your presentation or jump to any other document on your computer. An interactive project can include some of the content within the PowerPoint project and use hyperlinks to connect to Web pages with more details, Word documents with extensive rubrics formatted as tables, movies or sounds in formats that PowerPoint cannot recognize, etc.

To link to a Web page, choose the "Web Page" tab in Figure 2.8 (page 23) or "Existing File or Web Page" in Figure 2.9 (page 23). From there, simply type the URL (uniform resource locator; that's the Web address) in the box labeled "Address" or "Link to." Be sure to include the complete address (which generally starts with "http://"). Alternatively, click on the button labeled "Launch Web Browser" or the "Browse the Web" icon (it looks like a globe with a magnifying glass) to launch your Web browser. In some versions of PowerPoint, wherever you browse will automatically be inserted as the link; in other versions, you will have to copy the URL and paste it into PowerPoint. Note that if you have to paste and your Edit menu isn't active, you usually can use the keyboard shortcut (control-V in Windows or command-V on a Macintosh) to paste.

To link to another document, choose the "Document" tab in Figure 2.8 or "Existing File or Web Page" in Figure 2.9. Click on the "Locate . . . " button or the "Browse for File" icon (it looks like an open folder with an arrow opening it) to get the standard Open File dialog box. In Windows, you might have to pick files of type "All Files" to be sure you can see documents that PowerPoint does not recognize.

Note that when you are choosing a file, you are creating a link. Just like linked sounds, if you want PowerPoint to be able to open the document when the presentation is moved to another computer, you should put the file in the folder with your PowerPoint file before linking to it.

Buttons

Sometimes you want your users to click on text to follow a hyperlink, and sometimes you want them to click on a button. PowerPoint provides buttons with a few different icons for different purposes. Choose "Action Buttons" from the Slide Show menu, and a flyout menu will appear with either icons for buttons or names of buttons. Figure 2.10 shows the twelve different kinds of buttons: Custom, Home, Help, Information, Previous Slide, Next Slide, First Slide, Last Slide, Last Slide Viewed, Document, Sound, and Movie.

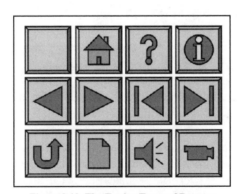

Figure 2.10. The Twelve Types of Buttons

The button icons do not have to correspond to the action the button will perform, but good rules of design dictate that the icon should make sense for what is going to happen when the button is pressed.

Once you select a button (from the flyout menu from "Action Buttons"), your cursor will change to a plus sign. You can either click on your slide and a standard size button will appear, or you can drag the mouse to create a button of any size you like. Don't worry if the size isn't perfect; you can always click on the button and drag it from the handles to change the size.

Once you create the button, you will be prompted with the dialog box shown in Figure 2.11.

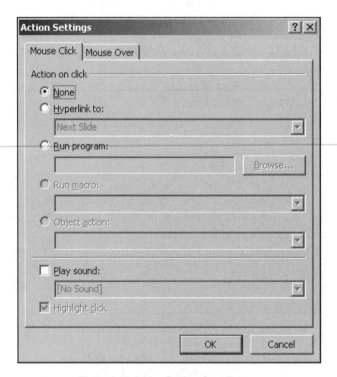

Figure 2.11. Action Settings for a Button

This dialog box allows you to have your button do many of the same things you could do with a hyperlink. Unfortunately, the same things are done in a slightly different way.

To link to another slide, you will choose "Hyperlink to" and pick from the drop-down menu. If you chose an icon for your button, "Hyperlink to" might already be chosen with PowerPoint's best guess for what you want to do. If PowerPoint guessed correctly, just click OK; otherwise pick something else.

Like the hyperlinks for text, you can choose "Next Slide," "Previous Slide," "First Slide," "Last Slide," and "Custom Show." You can also choose a specific slide by choosing "Slide . . . ," which will prompt you for the slide to link to.

In addition to the choices that were available for hyperlinks for text, you can also choose "Last Slide Viewed," which takes you to the slide that took you to the current slide. Imagine a quiz with several questions. Each wrong answer leads to a slide with the word "Wrong" (or some more gentle reminder that the incorrect answer was chosen) on it. The "Wrong" slide can contain a button that returns to the last slide viewed, so it always returns to the question that was just answered, no matter which question that is. Another additional option is "End Show," which will quit out of Slide Show View.

The "URL . . ." choice will allow you to type in a Web address, but it does not give you the option to browse for a Web address. "Other PowerPoint Presentation" not only lets you choose another PowerPoint file, but it also lets you pick which slide in that presentation the button will go to. Finally, "Other File . . ." is just like browsing for a file when choosing "Existing File or Web Page" or "Document" with a hypertext link.

Once you have chosen where to "Hyperlink to," click OK. If you ever want to change what the button does, click on the button to select it and choose "Action Settings" from the Slide Show menu.

Remember that buttons, like hyperlinks, only work in Slide Show View. If you click on them in Edit View, you will select them. Clicking on them in Slide Show View will do whatever action you set the button to do.

Now that you have seen a few things that buttons can do that hyperlinks cannot, I'll let you in on a little secret: Any PowerPoint object, including text, can have the same action settings as a button. If you click on a picture or a shape drawn with the Draw tools, or you highlight text, you can choose "Action Settings" from the Slide Show menu and get all the same options described in this section for buttons.

Text for Buttons

In some cases, an icon is enough to let the user know what the button does, but words are often clearer. Sometimes the best choice for a button is a "Custom" button (that's the blank one with no icon) and some text. To add text to a button, right-click on the button (control click on a Macintosh) and choose "Add Text." If the button already has text in it, you will have the option to "Edit Text" instead. You should see the cursor flashing inside your button waiting for you to type whatever text you want to appear in the button. This text can be formatted for font, size, style, and color, just like any text object.

If the text is too big to fit in the button, you can change the font size, or you can change the size of the button by dragging from the handles.

When a button has text, it is easy to change the action settings for the text instead of the entire button. Your clue that you have done this is that the text will change color and be underlined if it has action settings associated with it. Figure 2.12 (page 28) shows a menu button that has the link associated with the text, not the entire button.

Figure 2.12. Button with Action Settings for the Text

The problem with this is that if a user clicks anyplace on the button except the text, the button will not work. This situation can be even worse, if the button itself has action settings to do one thing, and the text of the button has action settings to do something else. If this happens, highlight the text in the button, choose "Action Settings" from the Slide Show menu, and click "None" for the action.

To be sure that you are setting your settings for the button itself and not just the text, click once on the button. If you see a flashing cursor in the text, click on the button again, but be sure to click somewhere outside of the text. Watch the shape of the cursor for the mouse. If it is the text cursor (known as the "I bar" because it looks like a capital I), then you are clicking in the text. Otherwise you are clicking outside of the text. Once you have selected the button, and not the text, you can choose "Action Settings" from the Slide Show menu.

Sound for Buttons

In Figure 2.11 (page 26), you will notice that you can check "Play Sound" at the bottom of the Action Settings dialog box. From the drop-down menu below that, you can choose from a few of the canned sounds that come with PowerPoint. You can also pick a sound file by choosing "Other Sound . . . " from the bottom of the list.

You might notice, however, that there is no option for recording your own sound. Because this is the most useful option for sounds for educational purposes, it is important to be able to do this. You might want a button to say where you are going when you click on it, you might want a button to read the text on a slide, or you might want to pronounce a vocabulary word when the word is clicked. This is all possible in PowerPoint.

Earlier in this chapter you learned how to record a sound to place it into your presentation by choosing "Movies and Sounds" from the Insert menu. Unfortunately, you did not have a choice about the icon used for the sound. The icon was always a little speaker. Perhaps you can compromise and use that icon instead of a button, but that will not work for vocabulary words. The solution is to add the sound with the speaker icon and then delete the icon. Remember that I warned you to always give your sound a sensible name when recording it? Now is the time you will use that name. Once you have recorded a sound, it is part of the presentation. It remains part of the presentation even if you delete the icon that plays the sound.

If you want a sound associated with a button, word, or any other PowerPoint object, perform the following steps:

1. Go to the Insert menu, choose "Movies and Sounds," and choose "Record Sound" from the flyout menu.

2. Record the sound as described in the "Sounds" section earlier in this chapter. Be sure to give the sound a name other than "Recorded Sound."

3. Click once on the sound icon to select it and hit the Delete or Backspace key on your keyboard to delete the icon.

4. Select the object or text you want associated with the sound and choose "Action Settings" from the Slide Show menu.

5. Check the "Play Sound" check box and choose your sound from the drop down menu. Your sound will be listed with the name you gave it. Note that you might have to scroll up or down to find your sound, as it might be in the list in alphabetical order or at the top of the list of sounds.

Controlling Navigation with Kiosk Mode

Now that you can create buttons and hyperlinks to take users where you want them to go, you might not want them to go anywhere you don't specify. Normally in PowerPoint, a mouse click, the space bar, the right arrow, and the Page Down key all move you to the next slide. If you have carefully planned choices for the users, you don't want them to mess that up by clicking and going to the next slide. The solution is Kiosk mode.

Choose "Set Up Show" from the Slide Show menu to get the dialog box shown in Figure 2.13 (page 30). In this dialog box, click on "Browsed at a Kiosk (full screen)." You now have complete control over the user. The only navigation key that will work when in Slide Show View is the Escape key, which will exit the show. This means that you must have buttons or hyperlinks to do anything. You cannot rely on the user to click the mouse anywhere to advance to the next slide because that will only work if the user clicks on a button.

One difficulty with Kiosk mode is animation. Animation in PowerPoint can be automatic or manual. Automatic animation works fine with Kiosk mode. Manual animation does not. If the user has to click or hit the space bar to activate animation (such as to have the next line of a bulleted list fly in from the left), this will be blocked by Kiosk mode. The solution is to make all your animation automatic.

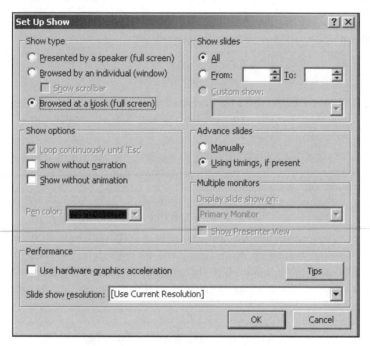

Figure 2.13. Selecting Kiosk Mode

If you choose to animate text, whether or not you use Kiosk mode, you should animate your navigation buttons as well. Have them appear on the screen after all the text has appeared. By doing this, users won't click a button to go to another slide before all the text has shown up on the current slide.

Saving As a PowerPoint Show

Once you have created a presentation for others to use, you do not necessarily want them to edit the presentation or even look at it in Edit or Normal View. You might want to save your presentation as a PowerPoint Show. If you double-click on a normal PowerPoint file, it will open in Edit or Normal View, where you can scroll through all the slides and edit them. If you double-click on a PowerPoint Show, it will open in Slide Show View. In addition, when you exit the show (by getting to the end of the show, hitting the Escape key on the keyboard, or clicking on a button tied to the "End Show" action), a PowerPoint Show will quit out of PowerPoint altogether and not return to Edit or Normal View.

To save a presentation as a PowerPoint Show, choose "Save As . . . " from the File menu and pay attention to the "Save as type." If you choose "PowerPoint Show," it will create a .pps file (see Figure 2.14). If you want to edit a PowerPoint Show, open the show from within PowerPoint, that is, start PowerPoint and choose "Open" from the File menu to open it.

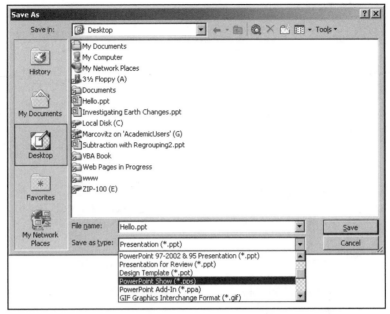

Figure 2.14. Saving a File As a PowerPoint Show

Conclusion

Now you have a basic understanding of the traditional interactive and multimedia features of PowerPoint. You are no longer confined to creating linear presentations that simply go from one slide to the next to the next. You have the full power of buttons and hyperlinks to allow for any of the designs described in Chapter 1 and, with Kiosk mode, you have complete control over where the user goes within your presentation. Now that you have conquered the traditional interactive multimedia features of PowerPoint, you are ready for the next chapter, which will introduce you to the advanced scripting features available to you in PowerPoint.

Exercises to Try

✍ Create a simple tutorial with a title slide, a menu slide, and four content sections. Put a button on your title slide to go to the menu slide. Link the menu to each of the content slides. Include a button on each of the content slides to return to the menu. Put your tutorial in Kiosk mode and save it as a PowerPoint Show. See Figure 2.15.

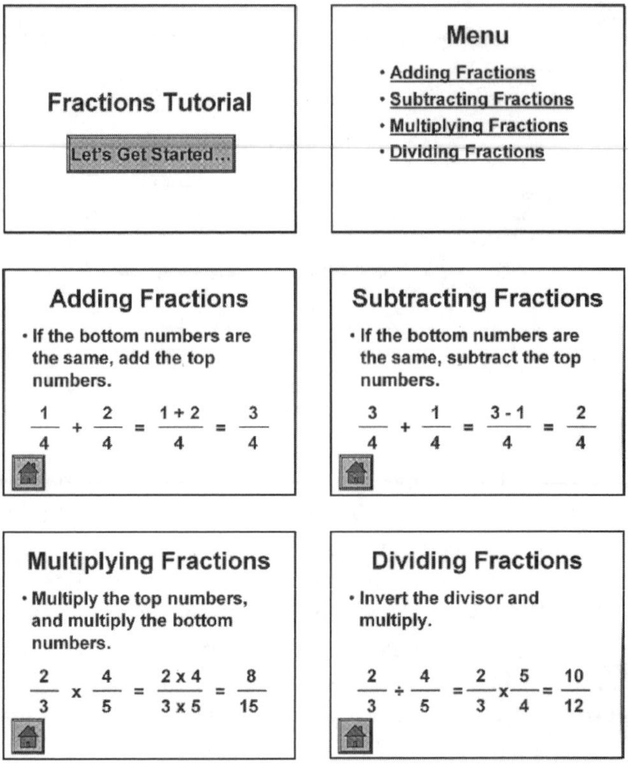

Fractions Tutorial

Let's Get Started...

Menu
- Adding Fractions
- Subtracting Fractions
- Multiplying Fractions
- Dividing Fractions

Adding Fractions
- If the bottom numbers are the same, add the top numbers.

$$\frac{1}{4} + \frac{2}{4} = \frac{1+2}{4} = \frac{3}{4}$$

Subtracting Fractions
- If the bottom numbers are the same, subtract the top numbers.

$$\frac{3}{4} + \frac{1}{4} = \frac{3-1}{4} = \frac{2}{4}$$

Multiplying Fractions
- Multiply the top numbers, and multiply the bottom numbers.

$$\frac{2}{3} \times \frac{4}{5} = \frac{2 \times 4}{3 \times 5} = \frac{8}{15}$$

Dividing Fractions
- Invert the divisor and multiply.

$$\frac{2}{3} \div \frac{4}{5} = \frac{2}{3} \times \frac{5}{4} = \frac{10}{12}$$

Figure 2.15. Slides for Tutorial with Menu

✍ Create a simple multiple-choice quiz with three questions. Create a slide for each question with buttons for right and wrong answers. Wrong-answer buttons should link to a slide that says "Wrong" and has a button that returns to the "Last Slide Viewed." Right-answer buttons should link to the next question and play a positive sound (such as applause or your recorded voice saying "good job") . Put your quiz in Kiosk mode and save it as a PowerPoint Show.

Introducing Visual Basic for Applications

Introduction

In Chapter 2 you learned some of the traditional multimedia features of PowerPoint, such as pictures, sounds, hyperlinks, and action buttons. These are important features of PowerPoint, and even if you become a VBA expert, you will use these features over and over again. But you might be wondering what VBA is and what it can do for you. This chapter explains what VBA is, describes how VBA fits into the world of object-oriented computer languages, and relieves your concerns about VBA and computer viruses.

Vocabulary

- Class
- Inheritance
- Macro virus protection
- Method
- Object
- Object-oriented programming language
- OOP
- Parameter
- Property
- VBA
- Virus
- Visual Basic for Applications

What Is Visual Basic for Applications?

Visual Basic for Applications (VBA) is a very powerful object-oriented programming language that can be used to add to the functionality of Microsoft Office applications, including Microsoft PowerPoint. You might have gotten stuck on the phrase "powerful object-oriented programming language." Don't let that bother you. Your car is a powerful electrical, mechanical, and thermodynamic transportation device, but you can still drive (or if you are too young to drive, your parents can drive, so how hard can it be?). Later in this chapter, you'll learn what it means to be a "powerful object-oriented programming language," but remember the premise of this book: You are learning to be a scripter, not a programmer. Just like you don't need to understand the thermodynamics of the combustion engine to drive your car, you can become a scripter without a degree in computer science.

Originally, PowerPoint was a presentation tool, used by many to enhance lectures, sometimes making them better and sometimes making them worse. PowerPoint served as an automated overhead projector. Slides could be changed with the click of a button. Pictures and sounds could be added. Text could fly onto the screen as points were introduced, saving the need for a piece of paper to cover half the projector (and annoy half the audience).

Enter PowerPoint 97. Starting with that version, PowerPoint was transformed from a presentation tool to an interactive tool. While it still can be used as a presentation tool, it becomes more powerful as an interactive tool. As you saw in Chapter 2, in addition to multimedia elements (pictures, sounds, videos), newer versions of PowerPoint allow interactive elements, including buttons and hyperlinks. You can

- add buttons to control navigation (start your slide show with a menu, for example, rather than requiring linear navigation, from slide to slide to slide);
- jump to other slide shows, files, or Web pages; and
- create rudimentary multiple-choice tests (clicking on a button with the correct answer takes the student to a slide that says "correct," for example).

While PowerPoint's interactivity is very powerful and useful, it is also very limited. VBA extends this to nearly unlimited dimensions. With VBA, you can change the content and appearance of slides based on student input, you can ask for and process typed input, you can add additional slides, you can hide and show graphics, and much more. You will learn the basics of scripting in VBA beginning in Chapter 4. First, we'll pause to learn a little bit about what object-oriented programming is.

Note that the VBA features of PowerPoint work in all versions of PowerPoint starting with version 97, but they do not work in the PowerPoint Viewer or when saved as a Web page. PowerPoint presentations that use VBA can be placed on the Web, but they must be downloaded from the Web and run directly on a machine with a full version of PowerPoint.

What Is an Object-Oriented Programming Language?

First of all, VBA is a programming language. Don't let this scare you . . . too much. Having a background in computer science and programming would be helpful, and you will not be able to take full advantage of VBA without becoming (at least) a novice programmer. However, this book guides you through some of the basic things you might want to do with VBA without the need of any programming background.

To top it off, VBA isn't just an ordinary programming language; it is an object-oriented programming (OOP) language. An OOP language has three key features: classes, objects, and methods. Classes are types of things, objects are specific things, and methods are what you do to things. For example, there is a class of things called "phone books." The specific phone book on my desk is an object. I can do many things with a phone book, such as look up a person's phone number, turn to a page, put it on a chair for my four-year-old daughter to sit on, etc. All the things that I could do to the phone book are methods. If we convert this phone book example to computerese (computerese is not a real computer language, but it plays one on TV), we might have the following:

```
Dim myPhoneBook As PhoneBook
myPhoneBook.LookUpPerson("John Smith")
```

The first line says that `myPhoneBook` is a specific instance (an object) of the class `PhoneBook`. This tells us that all the things we can do with phone books in general can be done to this specific phone book. Since one of the things that we can do with phone books is look up a specific person, we do that on the second line. `myPhoneBook.LookUpPerson` says that for this specific phone book, call the method (do the action) `LookUpPerson`. Since we need to know which person to look up, this method takes an argument (information that the method needs to complete its job). That information is put in parentheses after the method. Since the information is text, we put it in quotes, too.

Computers are very picky. All the details are important. The dot (that period between `myPhoneBook` and `LookUpPerson`) is necessary to tell the computer that `LookUpPerson` is the thing to do (method) with the object `myPhoneBook`. The parentheses tell the computer that the stuff inside is important information (parameters) for knowing what the method should do. The quotes tell the computer that what's inside them is text. Leave out any detail, and nothing will work.

Another critical point about objects is that they can have parts. Think about our phone book example. Think about what parts there are to a phone book. Here are a few examples: the cover, pages, the blue pages (for government listings), and the phone company information (such as how to contact the phone company if your phone stops working). Each of these parts is its own object (a particular page might be an example of the class `Page`, or a range of pages might be an example of the class `Pages`). You might access the phone book by accessing a part of the book. For example,

```
myPhoneBook.Pages.TurnToTheNextPage
```

might take the set of pages and turn them to the next one, so if you are on page 57, for example, you will find yourself on page 59 (if the page is two-sided). Now the dot is serving two purposes. The first dot says that `Pages` is a part of the object `myPhoneBook`, and the second dot tells the computer to do the thing (run the method) `TurnToTheNextPage`, which is something that can be done to `Pages`.

While some parts of an object are other objects, some parts are properties. For example, a phone book has a color, a number of pages, and a thickness. So for example, if I wanted to see how thick my phone book is, I might look at that property:

```
myPhoneBook.thickness
```

or I might want to add two thicknesses together to get something tall enough for my daughter to sit on and be able to reach the table:

```
myPhoneBook.thickness + myNeighborsPhoneBook.thickness
```

Finally, we turn to inheritance, and then you won't be an expert in OOP, but you will be able to play one on TV. We have been looking at the class `PhoneBook`. Well, isn't a phone book just a specific type of book? Therefore, we could think of a `PhoneBook` as a type of `Book` that inherits all the properties and methods from books. The object I am working with is still `myPhoneBook`, but it is not only a member of the class `PhoneBook`, it is (since `PhoneBook` is a subclass of `Book`) also a member of the class `Book`. Everything you can do with a book, in general, you can do with a phone book . . . and more. For example, you can turn pages in a book, look at the cover, weigh down papers, etc. You can also look up a phone number or find information about area codes in a phone book, but not in all books.

Now, with this basic understanding of objects, classes, and methods, you will be able to understand the basics of OOP when these terms come up.

Before leaving OOP, think about how it relates to PowerPoint. PowerPoint has many objects and classes. A typical PowerPoint presentation contains many slides. Slides! That's a class. As a class, Slides is the collection of all the individual slides in a presentation. The set of slides in your specific presentation is an object. That set of slides contains individual slides. A slide might contain many objects or shapes. Think about a slide with a text box, a piece of clip art, and a button. Perhaps these are shapes 1, 2, and 3 on the slide. They each have many properties, such as whether or not they are visible. Because a text box, a piece of clip art, and a button are all members of the class Shape and shapes may be visible or not, we can look at the Visible property of these objects. For example:

```
ActivePresentation.Slides(3).Shapes(2).Visible
```

This looks at the current PowerPoint presentation ActivePresentation. That presentation contains slides ActivePresentation.Slides. We want to look at the third slide (that's the 3 in parentheses), and we want to look at the second shape on that slide (Shapes(2)). Finally, that shape, like all shapes, can be visible or not, so we want to look at the Visible property. So, what that small piece of code says is: Look at the Visible property of the second shape, which is one of the shapes, on the third slide, which is one of the slides, in the current PowerPoint presentation. It's a good thing we can use VBA because we would get pretty tired typing out long sentences like that.

If you don't understand the details of object-oriented programming languages, don't worry. Because you are learning to be a scripter, you will be able to pick it up as you go along. The more you understand, the easier it will be to change scripts to suit your purposes, but to start, you only need to type the scripts you see.

VBA and Viruses

VBA is a powerful programming environment. It can do almost anything that can be done to your computer, including creating, deleting, or modifying files. It can access other programs, such as Outlook Express (an e-mail program). These features have been used to create and spread computer viruses and worms that destroy files and spread them to other computers. You could, for example, write a VBA program that deletes some important system files (making it impossible for the computer to start) and mails itself to others through e-mail. This has been done, and it affects you in two ways. First, once you learn enough VBA (and it doesn't take that much), you could do this. Don't!!! Don't even play around with this. It is inappropriate, unethical, and in many cases illegal.

Second, and more relevant to you (since I'm sure you wouldn't entertain the thought of writing viruses), some virus protection systems might look askance at your legitimate work. The thing you are most likely to see is PowerPoint's macro protection. This can be found in different places in different versions of PowerPoint. In all versions of PowerPoint, you start by going to the Tools menu and choosing "Options . . . ".

In older versions of PowerPoint (including PowerPoint 97), under the General tab, there is a checkbox for Macro virus protection. If this is checked, you will be asked if it is OK to enable macros every time you run a PowerPoint slide show or even open a PowerPoint project that contains anything done with VBA (see Figure 3.1).

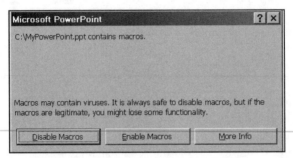

Figure 3.1. Do You Want to Enable Macros?

In newer versions of PowerPoint (including PowerPoint 2002), under the Security tab, there is a button for "Macro security . . . " (see Figure 3.2).

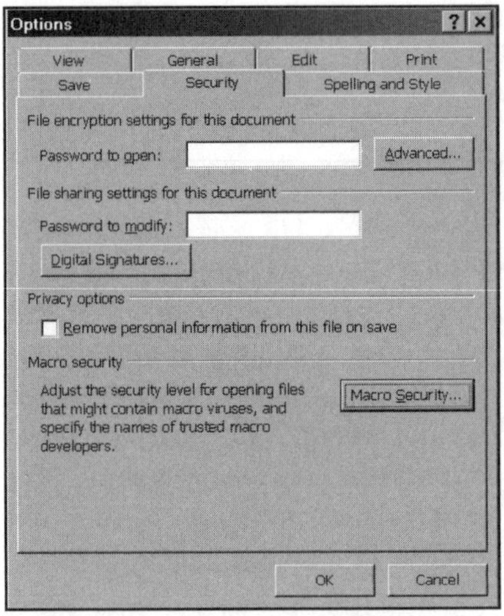

Figure 3.2. Security Tab Under Options

Click this button to bring up the Macro Security dialog box (see Figure 3.3). You can choose high, medium, or low security. If you choose high security, you will not be able to use VBA. Medium security is probably your best choice. You will be able to run PowerPoint presentations that contain VBA, but you will be asked if you want to enable macros before PowerPoint opens the presentation (see Figure 3.1). With low security, you will be able to open all PowerPoint presentations without being asked if you want to enable macros.

Be careful when you click on the "Enable Macros" button. If the slide show was written by you or someone you trust, choose Enable Macros. If not, it is generally a good idea to choose Disable Macros because some unscrupulous person might have included a virus in your file. Your students, when running your presentation, will have to choose Enable Macros.

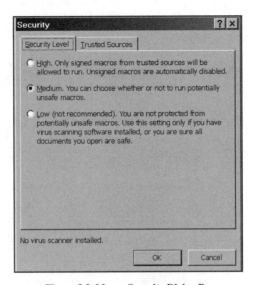

Figure 3.3. Macro Security Dialog Box

Conclusion

You now have a basic understanding of what VBA is and how it fits into the world of object-oriented programming languages. You also know the relationship between VBA scripts and macro viruses (although you would never use VBA for nefarious purposes). You are now ready to learn how to write VBA scripts.

Exercises to Try

✎ If you use a newer version of PowerPoint, set your macro security to medium or low. If you use an older version of PowerPoint, enable macro protection.

✎ Look at a simple PowerPoint presentation that you have created in the past. Using pencil and paper (or a drawing program or an organization chart slide in PowerPoint), try to draw a chart of all the parts of the presentation. Put the presentation at the top (you can call it ActivePresentation and put the collection of slides below that. Under the collection of slides, put each of your individual slides (if you chose a big presentation, just pick the first three or four slides). Under each slide, put the various objects on the slide. See Figure 3.4 if you are having trouble getting started. Don't worry if you don't get all the objects; the purpose of this exercise is to begin to think about all the objects that you will be able to manipulate with VBA.

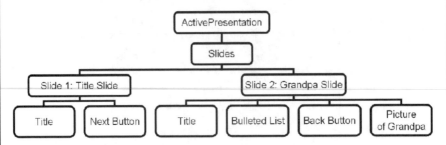

Figure 3.4. Example Chart of the Parts of a PowerPoint Presentation

✍ Pick one object from one slide and list as many properties as you can. The purpose of this exercise is not to get a detailed list of everything about a presentation or an individual object but to start thinking about how a presentation is organized and what properties objects might have for you to manipulate. Don't worry if you can't think of all the properties (objects contain properties about which you don't even know) or even if your properties don't match PowerPoint's "official" properties. To get you started, think about a rectangle's size, location, and color. You might also select the object within PowerPoint and try to see what properties you can change (click on the object to select it, go to the Format menu, and choose the last item in the menu, which will be the type of object you are formatting, i.e., "Picture" if the object is a picture, "Text Object" if the object is a text object, "AutoShape" if the object is a drawn shape, etc.). Anything you can change with traditional PowerPoint features you will be able to change with VBA.

Getting Started with VBA

Introduction

In previous chapters you learned some basic features of PowerPoint and what VBA is. This chapter shows you how to access the VBA Editor, how to write simple scripts in VBA, how to attach those scripts to buttons and objects, and how to protect your scripts with a password. When you have completed this chapter, you will know the mechanics of writing a script and using it in a PowerPoint presentation, and you will be ready to learn how to do some interesting things with VBA.

Vocabulary

- Action settings
- Add Text
- Button
- Macro

- Module
- MsgBox
- Password
- Visual Basic Editor

Accessing the VBA Editor

Once you start a PowerPoint project, you get into VBA by holding down the ALT key and hitting the F11 key (option-F11 on a Macintosh). Alternatively, go to the Tools menu, choose "Macro," and choose "Visual Basic Editor" from the flyout menu. At this point, you should see two small windows on the left (the Project window and the Properties window) and a large blank area on the right of the screen. Choose "Module" from the Insert menu, and you will get a window in the blank area (see Figure 4.1). The window probably will be named "Module1." This is where you will write your procedures.

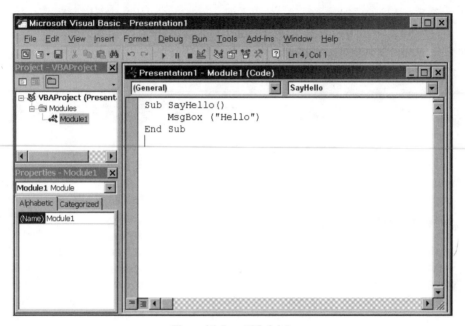

Figure 4.1. Insert Module1

While we are here, let's write one. Type the following:

```
Sub SayHello()
   MsgBox("Hello")
End Sub
```

Note that the computer will type the "End Sub" for you. Now go to the Run menu, and select "Run Sub/UserForm." You should get a message box that says Hello (see Figure 4.2).

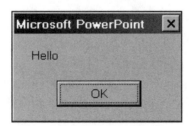

Figure 4.2. MsgBox Says "Hello"

Congratulations! You have just written and executed your first VBA procedure. Click the OK button, and you can do some more.

Help! I've Lost My Windows

You're adventurous. You like to play around. You were trying some things, and you lost your Project window in the VBA Editor. No problem. Keep playing around; it is the best way to learn. Oh yeah, and you want to get your Project window back. Simply go to the View menu and choose "Project Explorer." What's that? You lost your module window, too? You *are* adventurous. Just double-click on Module1 in the Project Window, as shown in Figure 4.3.

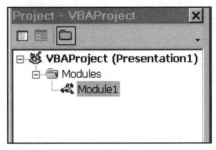

Figure 4.3. Project Window with Module1

If you don't see Module1 in the Project window, but you do see Modules, you should have a + next to Modules; click on that and you should see Module1. If you don't see Modules, but you do see VBAProject, you should have a + next to VBAProject; click on that to see Modules, click on the + next to Modules to see Module1, and double-click on Module1 to see the Module1 window. Finally, if you don't see Modules, and you don't see a + next to VBA Project, then you don't have a module (either you never inserted it, or you deleted it). Go to the Insert menu, and choose "Module," and you should be OK.

If you accidentally add more than one module, your modules will be numbered consecutively (Module1, Module2, Module3, . . .). While it is not a problem to have more than one module, you should avoid confusion by keeping all your scripts in the same module. Delete any extra modules by clicking on them in the Project window and choosing "Delete Module" from the File menu.

Tying Your VBA Script to a PowerPoint Button

Now that you have a script written, you will want to access it from within PowerPoint. You can do this by associating the script with a button (or any drawing shape that you want).

Go to PowerPoint (either choose it from the Task Bar or close the Visual Basic Editor by clicking on the ⊠ in the upper right-hand corner of the screen; on a Macintosh, choose "Close and Return to Microsoft PowerPoint" from the File menu). Don't worry about losing your VBA scripts when you close the editor. Your VBA scripts are part of your PowerPoint presentation. When you save your presentation, your scripts will be saved with it. When you return to the editor, your scripts will still be there.

If you don't have a slide, create a blank slide. Don't worry about what kind of slide it is or what is on it. Go to the Slide Show menu and select "Action Buttons." From the flyout menu, pick any button (the blank one is fine because you can add text to it later). See Figure 4.4 to see how to add a blank action button.

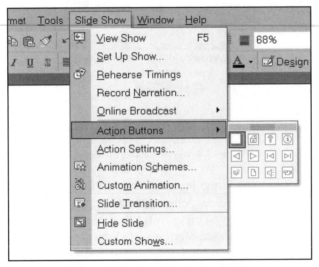

Figure 4.4. Getting a Blank Action Button

You can draw the button by dragging the mouse to form the button or just clicking where you want the button to appear on the slide. Once you let go of the mouse you will be presented with the Actions Settings dialog box (see Figure 4.5). Choose Run Macro, and select SayHello (the name of the procedure you just wrote) as the macro to run. Click OK.

Buttons are only active in Slide Show View, so go to Slide Show View (choose "View Show" from the Slide Show menu or click on the Slide Show icon 🖵 in the lower left corner of the screen). Now, click on your button, and you should get the same "Hello" message you got earlier when running your procedure (see Figure 4.2, page 42).

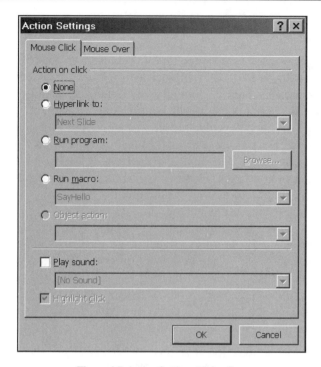

Figure 4.5. Action Settings Dialog Box

Now go back to Edit View (also known as Normal View) by hitting the Escape key on your keyboard. To finish your button, right-click (control click on a Macintosh) on it and choose "Add Text" from the flyout menu. You can now add text to describe what your button does. This text will show up on the button, so users will know what they are clicking when they click your button.

Tying Your VBA Script to Any Object

You can tie your VBA script to any object you want, not just a button. Use the drawing tools to draw a shape (there are several interesting ones from which to choose in the AutoShapes menu of the Draw toolbar). Once you have drawn the shape, click on it to select it. Now choose "Action Settings" from the Slide Show menu. You will get the same dialog box shown in Figure 4.5, and you can choose Run Macro and the SayHello macro, exactly as you did above. Now you can click on the drawn object just like you can click on the button.

This method works for any PowerPoint object, not just the ones you draw yourself. You can insert clip art and make it clickable by assigning Action Settings (just like you do to shapes you draw yourself) to run your script. You can copy and paste pictures from other sources (such as the Web). You can even make text in your slide clickable by highlighting the text and choosing "Action Settings" from the Slide Show menu.

Changing a Button

You might want to make three types of changes to your button: changing the PowerPoint attributes of a button, such as size shape, or text; changing which script a button uses (including adding a script if the button isn't tied to one); and changing what the script does that the button uses.

To change the attributes of a button, you would use traditional PowerPoint features. For example, you can change the text in the button by right-clicking on the button and choosing "Edit Text" ("Add Text" if the button doesn't already have any text) from the flyout menu. You can use any of the drawing tools to change the size, shape, color, etc., of the button.

If you created your button and didn't tie it to a script, you can right-click on the button and choose "Action Settings" from the flyout menu. Alternatively, you can left-click on the button to select it, go to the Slide Show menu, and choose "Action Settings." Once in the Action Settings dialog box (see Figure 4.5, page 45), you can choose Run Macro. If you had associated your button with the wrong script, you can change which script the button runs in the Action Settings dialog box. If you have more than one script, you can choose a different script from the pull-down menu under Run Macro. If you don't want your button to run any script, click None in the Action Settings dialog box.

Beware! If you have added text to your button, it is easy to accidentally link the text rather than the button. Generally, you want the entire button to activate your script, not just the text inside the button. You can tell that you have linked the text because PowerPoint will generally underline linked text. To ensure that you link the entire button, left click on the button to select it. Be sure that you do not have a cursor flashing in the text. If you do, left click anywhere on the button that is outside of the text. At this point you can either choose "Action Settings" from the Slide Show menu or right-click on the border of your button and choose "Action Settings" from the flyout menu. Because PowerPoint allows you to link text separately from a button, you easily can get confused. If you have linked the text and you later check to see which script the button activates, your Action Settings dialog box will indicate "None." Be careful to always link the entire button to avoid this confusion.

Securing Your VBA Script from Prying Eyes

In Chapter 2 we discussed Kiosk mode. By using Kiosk mode, you have put in place some security. Students will not be able to jump to any slide or skip a slide using the keyboard. However, you might put something in your VBA code that you don't want them to see. For example, if you are writing a quiz, your VBA code will include the answers so it can tell the students when they got the right and wrong answers. It is very easy to protect your VBA code with a password. While in the VBA Editor (where you edit the VBA code, not where you edit the PowerPoint slides), select "VBAProject Properties . . . " from the Tools menu and click on the Protection tab (see Figure 4.6).

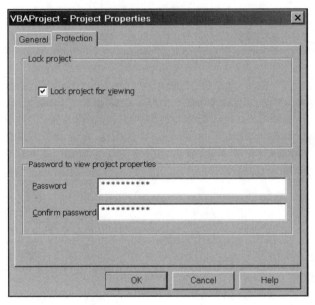

Figure 4.6. Setting a Password

Check the box that is labeled "Lock project for viewing," type a password in the password box, and type the same password in the "Confirm password" box. Now, whenever you want to view or edit the VBA code, you will be asked to type this password. Don't forget it, or you will not be able to access your own project.

Note that in newer versions of PowerPoint (beginning with 2002), you can set a password to access your file. If you choose to use this, beware of two things: (1) Anyone viewing your presentation will need the password, and (2) anyone using a version of PowerPoint earlier than 2002 will not be able to view your presentation.

Conclusion

You now have control over navigation, you know how to lock your scripts with a password, and you know the basics of writing VBA scripts. You are ready to learn some more sophisticated scripts to promote interactivity.

Exercises to Try

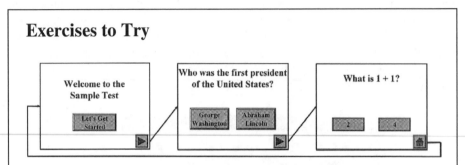

Figure 4.7. Slides for a Simple Quiz in the Chapter 4 Exercise

✎ Create a small multiple-choice quiz in PowerPoint. Include a title slide and two question slides with two answers for each question: one correct and one incorrect. The questions should be in a text object or the title area of a title only slide. The answers should be buttons.

✎ Use Add Text to add the text for the correct and incorrect answers to each question.

✎ Put a button on each slide to advance to the next slide.

✎ Put a button on the last slide to return to the title slide.

✎ Write a VBA script that is identical to SayHello, except name it RightAnswer. Replace the text "Hello" with the text "Good job."

✎ Write another VBA script that is identical to SayHello, except name it WrongAnswer. Replace the text "Hello" with the text "Try to do better next time."

✎ Link your answer buttons to the RightAnswer and WrongAnswer scripts.

✎ Save your file and run it in Slide Show View.

✎ Add a password to protect the VBA from being seen.

5

Let's Get Scripting

Introduction

In Chapter 4 you learned how to access the VBA Editor and write a simple script. In this chapter you will begin to learn a few more basic scripts, including some scripts that allow you to get input from the user. In the process, you will learn a little bit about variables, which are used to store information, so you can use it when you give feedback. What good would it be to ask for the user's name, if you don't use it as part of the feedback? You will get a preview of how to use some of the same scripts to get other kinds of input, such as answers to short-answer questions. Finally, in this chapter you will learn some details about running your scripts and associating them with buttons, including how to associate a button with more than one script.

Vocabulary

- Ampersand (&)
- Declare
- Dim
- InputBox
- Scope

- String
- Underscore
- Variable
- Variable type

Variables and Getting Input

Earlier, you used a `MsgBox` to pop up a message on the screen. You can use a similar box to get input from your students. The only difference is that the new dialog box will have a space for your students to type something. We'll start with something simple: asking for the student's name.

```
Sub YourName()
    userName = InputBox(Prompt:="Type your name", _
        Title:="Input Name")
End Sub
```

There are a few important things about this simple procedure. First, pay attention to the space and underscore at the end of the line. The last three characters on the second line are comma, space, and underscore. Without the space, the computer won't recognize the underscore that follows. The underscore is a special VBA character that tells VBA that what is on the next line is part of this line. Therefore that entire line could have been written on one line without the underscore:

```
userName = InputBox(Prompt:="Type your name", Title:="Input Name")
```

The underscore simply allows you to divide long lines so you don't have to scroll to the right to see what is on each line. Feel free to write long lines on one line or divide them up among several lines as you see fit.

The next thing that is important about this small piece of code is that it uses a variable: `userName`. Since we don't do anything with the variable at this point, it is not terribly interesting, but we should note a few things about variables. Variables are places to store information. You can think of them as boxes in the computer's memory. Unlike algebraic variables, which represent one (or more than one) specific, unchanging value in an equation or series of equations, computer variables change values. That is, you can take something out of a box and put something else into the box. In algebra, the equation

```
x = x + 1
```

would not make any sense. In the computer, it makes perfect sense for two reasons:

1. While the variable x can only hold one value at a time, that value can change. At one time x might hold the value 7, and a moment later, x might hold the value 8.

2. The equal sign (=) is not a statement of equality. It is an assignment operator. It says, take the value on the right side and store it in the variable named on the left side. Therefore, the above equation is not a statement of algebraic fact; it is an action. The part on the right $(x + 1)$ says, find what the value of x is and add one to it; the rest $(x =)$ says,

store that value in x. That is, if x was 7, it will now be 8. Using the box analogy, it says, look in the box we call "x," add one to what you find there, and put the result back in the box.

In the `YourName` procedure, we have used the variable `userName`. What we have said is: Take whatever the user types in the `InputBox` and put it into a variable called `userName`. Later, we will want to use the name (to say, for example, "Good job, Ella") so we will get it out of the `userName` box when we are ready.

 Note that `InputBox` does not work properly in PowerPoint 98 for the Macintosh. It works fine in all later Macintosh versions (PowerPoint 2001 and later) and in all Windows versions (PowerPoint 97 and later). If you are working in PowerPoint 98, you should probably upgrade to a later version. In the meantime, you can still work with the `InputBox` procedure. This is only a workaround and is not acceptable to give to students. If you create a button that uses an `InputBox`, the computer seems to freeze (your cursor changes to the watch). What is actually happening is that the computer has displayed the dialog for the `InputBox` where you can't see it. It is simply waiting for you to type your input. You can't see the box, you can't see the question, and you can't see the answer you type, but you can type an answer and hit the Return key when you are done. Fortunately, this does not affect Windows at all, and it only affects one version of PowerPoint for the Macintosh, and you can upgrade to a newer version that works fine.

Variable Declarations

For a variable to be useful, you often need to declare it. Although it is not necessary to declare all variables, it is good practice to do so. Declaring a variable does two things for you: It tells the computer what procedures are allowed to know about the variable (scope), and it tells the computer what kind of information the variable can hold (type). Declaring a variable is very easy. You do it with the `Dim` statement:

```
Dim userName
```

This line tells the computer that you want a box called `userName` to store some information (see Figure 5.1, page 52).

Figure 5.1. A Box Called `userName`

> **Beware!** All `Dim` statements must go together at the top of your module (or right after the `Sub` line in a procedure). Never put a `Dim` statement between procedures. If you add a new procedure that needs a new variable, put the procedure where you want, and put the `Dim` statement for the variable with the other `Dim` statements at the beginning of the module.

The most important part about the `Dim` statement is where to put it. You have two choices: You can put it at the beginning of your procedure (right after the `Sub` statement) or at the beginning of your module (before any `Sub` statements). If you put it any place else, it will not work. While programmers have lots of good reasons to put `Dim` statements in procedures, we are scripters, so for the purposes of this book, we will put most of our `Dim` statements at the beginning of the module. A `Dim` statement at the beginning of a module means that every procedure in the module can access that variable. That is, the scope of the variable is the entire module.

Alternatively, if you put the `Dim` statement at the beginning of the procedure, only that procedure can use the variable; that is, the scope of the variable is the procedure. For the `YourName` procedure, it would be pretty silly to create the `userName` variable so that only `YourName` could use it. If we did that, when we add a second procedure (such as the `DoingWell` procedure to tell the user how well he or she is doing), we won't be able to use the name typed by the user. That is, we would be stuck saying "Good job" instead of "Good job, Ada." Therefore, we want to add a `Dim` statement at the beginning of the module:

```
Dim userName

Sub YourName()
    userName = InputBox(Prompt:="Type your name", _
        Title:="Input Name")
End Sub
```

Just be sure that the Dim statement, along with all other Dim statements, is the first thing in your module regardless of where in the module the YourName procedure is.

Variable Types

Variables are of certain types. That is, certain variables can hold certain kinds of information. If you don't tell the computer what kind of information the variable is holding in advance, it will figure it out. In the YourName procedure, the function InputBox always returns a variable of type String (a String is text), so VBA will figure out that userName is a String. However, it is a good idea to be explicit and tell the computer that you want userName to be of type String. You can do this by changing the earlier Dim statement:

```
Dim userName As String
```

This Dim statement not only tells the computer that we want a variable called userName, but it also tells it what kind of information that variable can hold (using our box analogy, it tells it the size and shape of the box). In this case, our variable will hold a String (i.e., text) of up to 65,536 characters long.

Note that when you type a space after As, most versions of the VBA editor will try to suggest things for you to type with a little box that pops up (see Figure 5.2).

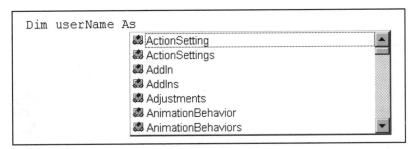

Figure 5.2. Variable Type Pop-Up Box

This box contains all the things that you can type now. Boxes like this will pop up frequently. If you know what you want to type, just ignore the box. If you're not sure what you want to type, scroll through the list to see the possibilities. If you find what you want on the list, you can either type it yourself or double-click on it in the box. When you double-click it will appear just as if you typed it, except that the computer will never spell it wrong.

For `Dim userName As`, you'll see all the types of things that `userName` can contain. There are about 300 of them, but there are just a few that you will care about now. Common types you will use are:

Boolean	True or False values
Integer	Any integer from –32,768 to 32,767
Long	Any integer from –2,147,483,648 to 2,147,483,647
Shape	Any PowerPoint shape (such as those things that can be drawn with the Draw tools)
Single	Non-integers (i.e., numbers with something after the decimal point, such as 3.14 and 98.6)
String	Any text up to 65,536 characters long
Object	Any object

Now, we are ready to put it all together with a `Dim` statement and two procedures:

```
Dim userName As String

Sub YourName()
   userName = InputBox(prompt:="Type your name", _
      Title:="Input Name")
End Sub

Sub DoingWell()
   MsgBox("You are doing well, " & userName)
End Sub
```

The first procedure could be associated with a button on the first slide, and the second procedure could be associated with a button on a later slide. The result would be that when the first button was pressed, the student would be asked to "Type your name." If the student types "Ada," when the second button is pressed, a message would pop up on the screen saying, "You are doing well, Ada." The & (ampersand) character used in the `MsgBox` procedure is for concatenation of strings; i.e., the two strings "You are doing well," and whatever is stored in the variable `userName` (in this case "Ada") are joined together to make one string, "You are doing well, Ada," which is displayed in the box on the screen.

Of course this is a simple example, but it is really easy to turn it into a multiple-choice quiz with feedback that uses the student's name. Figure 5.3 shows the VBA script and slides for a short quiz. The arrows show which button should be connected to which procedure. The Next buttons and Quit button do not use

VBA; they use traditional hyperlinks (see Chapter 2) for Next Slide and End Show. If you have forgotten how to tie your buttons to a procedure, look back in Chapter 4.

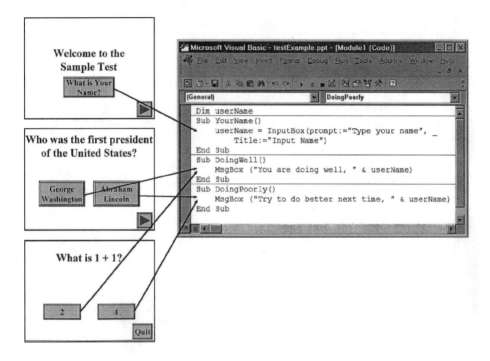

Figure 5.3. Simple Quiz

Force the Student to Type Something

Now, you have a nice procedure to ask for a name, but some students will not want to type their names. We have ways of making them type. Let's expand our procedure to what is shown in Figure 5.4 (page 55).

This example is a little more complicated than necessary (i.e., the same thing could have been done with four or five lines of code), but the complexity makes it easier to change. As a scripter, you always want to know what you can change. But first, let's try to understand what the procedure is doing. If you don't understand it all, don't worry; you can type the examples exactly as they are without understanding anything, and you can make small changes without understanding very much.

You should recognize the line beginning with userName =. That is the core of our old YourName procedure. The rest of the procedure is designed to figure out if the student has typed anything and, if not, ask the student again for a name.

```
Microsoft Visual Basic - Force.ppt - [Module1 (Code)]        _ □ ×
File  Edit  View  Insert  Format  Debug  Run  Tools  Add-Ins  Window  Help
                                                                 _ ₽ ×

(General)                           (Declarations)

    Dim userName
    Sub YourName()
        Dim done As Boolean

        done = False
        While Not done
            userName = InputBox(prompt:="Type your name", _
                Title:="Input Name")
            If userName = "" Then
                done = False
            Else
                done = True
            End If
        Wend
    End Sub
```

Figure 5.4. Ask For and Require a Name

To decide if the student has typed anything, we use a variable named done. When done is True, the user has typed something. When done is False, the user hasn't typed anything. You might notice that we declared this variable inside the procedure YourName. This means that only YourName will know about done (it would work just fine to declare done at the beginning of the module right before or after the Dim statement for userName). done is declared as Boolean because Boolean variables can be True or False, and we are either done or we are not done.

We start by setting the value of done to False (because the student surely has not typed a name before we even have asked). Next, we use a While loop (see Chapter 8 for more about While loops). This is a method of doing something over and over again as long as we want to keep going. We know we want to keep going if whatever comes after the word While is True. Not False is the same thing as True, so if done is False, Not done is True, and we keep going. In English, we keep going as long as we are not done.

How do we know when we are done? That is where the If statement comes in. We check to see what the student has typed (as stored in userName) and compare that to "" (that is two double quotes with nothing between them, also known as the empty string or nothing). If the student typed nothing (If username = "" Then) then we are not done, so we set done to False (done = False); that is, we put the value False in the variable named done. Otherwise (Else) the student must have typed something, so we are done, and we set done to True (done = True). The Wend just says that we are at the end of our While loop. Everything between the While and Wend will be executed over and over again until we are done (in this case, until the student types something).

If the user types nothing, the If statement will set done to False, and loop back up to the While statement. The While statement will see that we are not done, so we should keep going and execute the stuff between While and Wend again. If the user types something, the If statement will set done to True and loop back up to the While statement. The While statement will see that we are done and move to whatever is after the Wend (we could do something else after the Wend, but we don't in this example).

Two things to note:

1. Students will be forced to type something, but that something could be anything: a single space, a dirty word, a period, etc.

2. Students will only be forced to type something if they click on the button associated with this script.

In later chapters, you'll learn how to check what was typed to make sure it is OK, as well as how to force the student to click on the button (don't worry; it doesn't involve physical force or shock therapy).

What Else? A Personal Response and a Short-Answer Question

Now that you have a basic script that responds to what the student typed, we can extend it just a little to give a more personal response. Then with almost no effort, we can change the script from asking for a name to asking for the answer to a short-answer question.

The first step is to add ElseIf to the YourName procedure.

```
Sub YourName()
   Dim done As Boolean

   done = False
   While Not done
      userName = InputBox(prompt:="Type your name", _
         Title:="Input Name")
      If userName = "" Then
         done = False
      ElseIf userName = "Emily" Then
         MsgBox("Finish your homework before doing this.")
         done = False
      Else
         done = True
      End If
   Wend
End Sub
```

After we ask the question about the student typing nothing, we ask one more question. So first, we check to see if userName is nothing. If it isn't, we ask if userName is "Emily." If userName isn't nothing, and it isn't Emily, then we look at what comes after Else. If userName is "Emily," we have two things to do: put up a message telling Emily to do her homework, and set done to False. Because done is False (just like it would be if the student typed nothing), we'll ask for the name again.

This could be expanded to ask as many questions as you want by adding more ElseIf questions. Each one could check for a different name (or an unacceptable answer, like profanity) and respond appropriately. Note that ElseIf does not have a space between "Else" and "If" while End If does have a space between "End" and "If."

Using the exact same structure, we can change this from asking for a student's name to asking for the answer to a question. The main structure of the VBA looks like this:

```
Sub Question()
    Dim done As Boolean

    done = False
    While Not done
        answer = InputBox(prompt:="What color is the sky?", _
            Title:="Question")
        If answer = "" Then
            done = False
        ElseIf answer = "blue" Then
            MsgBox("Good job.")
            done = True
        Else
            MsgBox("Try Again.")
            done = False
        End If
    Wend
End Sub
```

You should notice that this is almost identical to YourName, with the following exceptions:

- We changed the name of the procedure; you can name procedures anything you want as long as they make sense to you.

- We changed the name of the variable; you can name variables anything you want as long as they make sense to you.

- We changed the text in the InputBox; as a scripter, you always should look for text between quotes that you can change.

- We changed the text in the ElseIf line to check to compare what was typed to the right answer; remember, as a scripter, you should be looking to change the text for the question and the text for the answer to whatever you want.

- We changed the `done = False` to `done = True` after `ElseIf` and `done = True` to `done = False` after `Else`; this is because you are done (`done = True`) when you get the right answer.

- Finally, we added some feedback. If what was typed wasn't nothing and it wasn't the right answer, we pop up a `MsgBox` to tell the student to try again.

Think about the small differences between the `YourName` and `Question` procedures. As a scripter, you should think about ways to change a script to make it do something different. Simply changing some text should be easy for you. Transforming `YourName` into `Question` might be a bit difficult at this point, but with practice, you should be able to find more and more things that you can change.

Running Your Scripts

Before we write any more procedures, you should be reminded how to run procedures. There are three ways to run a procedure:

1. Select "Run Sub/UserForm" from the Run menu in the VBA Editor.

2. Associate your procedure with a button so it runs when the user clicks on it in Slide Show View.

3. Call the procedure from another procedure.

Generally, we won't use method 1. Although it will work for some of the simple scripts we have written so far, it will not work for most of our scripts because we will design our scripts to be run in Slide Show View. When we choose "Run Sub/UserForm," we are not in Slide Show View.

Most of the time, we will use method 2, associate the procedure with a button. We did this at the beginning of Chapter 4. Remember that procedures aren't magic; they have to be told to run. The best way to tell them to run is to associate them with a button and to click on that button in Slide Show View.

Sometimes we will want to use method 3. In this method we write one script that includes the names of other scripts in it. Our button will be associated with the first script, but when that script is run, the other scripts will run as well. The next section describes this in more detail.

Calling a Procedure from Another Procedure

Not all procedures are tied directly to buttons. Many procedures are designed to do part of what you want a button to do. These procedures are called from other procedures. For example, let's take two procedures we have already written: `YourName` and `DoingWell` (for simplicity we'll use our first `YourName` procedure, but you could use any of the `YourName` procedures from this chapter):

```
Dim userName As String
Sub YourName()
  userName = InputBox(prompt:="Type your name", _
    Title:="Input Name")
End Sub

Sub DoingWell()
   MsgBox("You are doing well, " & userName)
End Sub
```

You could associate a button with each of these procedures, so the users click on the first button to type their names and (probably at some later point) click on the other button to be told how well they are doing. What if we want to praise them right away, to encourage them right after they have typed a name? We could write another procedure that calls the two procedures above:

```
Sub YourNameWithPraise()
   YourName
   DoingWell
End Sub
```

No buttons have to be associated with YourName or DoingWell. Create a button and associate it with YourNameWithPraise, and that is all you need. The button will activate YourNameWithPraise. When YourNameWithPraise starts to execute it will see the first line: YourName. That signals it to run the YourName procedure. When it finishes the YourName procedure, it will run DoingWell. Your module will look like Figure 5.5.

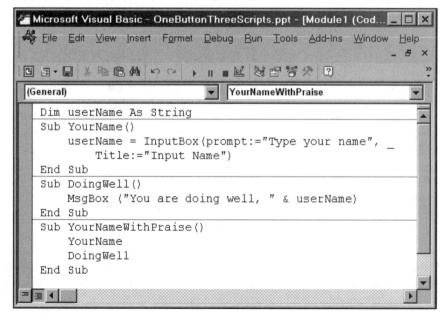

Figure 5.5. YourNameWithPraise Calls YourName and DoingWell

Conclusion

You now have learned a few basic scripts to interact with your students. You can get input and use it in feedback, either to include a student's name in the feedback or to judge a short-answer question. In the next chapter you will expand your bag of VBA tricks, including ways to manipulate your PowerPoint slides, such as moving from slide to slide and hiding objects on your slides.

Exercises to Try

↪ If you completed the "Exercise to Try" in Chapter 4, edit your presentation to change the RightAnswer and WrongAnswer scripts to include the student's name. Be sure to add a button on the first slide, to ask for the student's name (using the YourName procedure in this chapter).

↪ Add another slide to your quiz with a short-answer question. Put a single button on the slide that pops up the question. Use a different question than the one in this chapter. Don't worry if you can't figure this out. Chapter 7 includes detailed instructions on how to do this.

6

A Scripting Bag of Tricks

Introduction

In Chapter 5 you began to expand your single trick (the `MsgBox`) into a small bag of tricks. On the way you learned some important lessons about variables, loops, and `If` statements. With this, you have the power to do some interesting things to your PowerPoint projects. You can create an interactive multimedia extravaganza as long as you only want it to be a little interactive. In this chapter, you'll expand your bag of tricks to include several interactive features including navigation (i.e., moving around from slide to slide); hiding and showing PowerPoint objects; and changing text, font, size, and style in objects. You'll finish off the chapter with an example that ties some of the tricks together: You'll create a simple mystery with a clue sheet on which users can keep track of clues.

Vocabulary

- Comment
- Constant
- Initialize
- Navigation
- `With` Block

- Placeholder
- Property
- RGB
- TextRange

Comments

Starting in this chapter, our examples are going to get a little more complicated. That makes this a good time to talk about comments. So far, any explanation of the VBA code has been placed in the text, but it might be helpful to have some explanation built right into the code. This will be useful for me to explain things to you, and it will be useful for you to explain things to yourself. Comments are good at the beginning of procedures, as a brief note at the end of a line, and as a note inside a procedure. In addition, comments are helpful to point out obvious things because what is obvious to me might not be obvious to you, and what is obvious to you now might not make as much sense when you look at it later. And comments are helpful to point out things that are not obvious. A line like

```
If answer = "" Then
```

obviously checks to see if the variable answer contains nothing, but it might be helpful to put a comment, such as "The user didn't type anything."

```
If answer = "" Then 'The user didn't type anything.
```

The comment starts with a single quote. This tells the computer to ignore everything else on the line. That is, comments are for people looking at VBA code, not for computers running VBA code; the computer ignores the comments. As in this example, the comment can appear at the end of a line, or it can appear on a line by itself or even on several lines each starting with a single quote:

```
'This procedure is our very first procedure.
'It puts a message on the user's screen that says "Hello."
Sub SayHello()
   MsgBox("Hello") 'This is the line that puts up the message.
End Sub
```

If you type this example into your VBA Editor, you will notice that the comments turn green. That will help you distinguish VBA code for the computer from comments for you.

The next section discusses how VBA can be used to move from one slide to another. This is an excellent place for a comment. The VBA command will tell you that you are moving to slide 3, for example, but it won't tell you why. If, for example, slide 3 is your menu, a comment that says "Returning to the main menu" will help you understand what your script is supposed to do.

Navigation: Moving from Slide to Slide

The traditional features of PowerPoint that you have used include the ability of moving from one slide to another with action buttons or hypertext links. If you hadn't seen this before, you learned about it in Chapter 2. In fact, almost anywhere you can go with VBA you can go with traditional PowerPoint hyperlinks. So why would you want to complicate your life by doing something with VBA that you already can do without it? This is a trick question. While you can link to the same places without VBA, your hyperlinks only work when you click a button or text, and linking will be the only thing that button or text does. With VBA, you can link and do something else, or you can link to different places depending upon the answer to a question (using something like what we did in Chapter 5 with the YourName procedure or the Question procedure).

At the end of Chapter 5 you saw the procedure YourNameWithPraise. This procedure did two things: It asked for the student's name and it said, "You are doing well." Let's start with that and make one small addition:

```
Sub YourNameWithPraise()
    YourName
    DoingWell
    ActivePresentation.SlideShowWindow.View.Next
End Sub
```

The line that we added moves to the next slide. Don't worry how it does it; just remember that any time you want to use VBA to move to the next slide, you can insert that line into your procedure.

Imagine a title slide of your presentation. The only button on the slide would be associated with this procedure (of course, you would need the YourName and DoingWell procedures in your module, but only YourNameWithPraise would be tied directly to a button). When the user clicks on the button, YourName is called (the user is asked to type a name), DoingWell is called (the user is told by name, "You are doing well") and the presentation automatically begins by moving to the next slide.

Of course, you don't always want to go to the next slide. To move around within your presentation, you can use any of the following:

`ActivePresentation.SlideShowWindow.View.GotoSlide (3)`	Go to slide 3
`ActivePresentation.SlideShowWindow.View.GotoSlide (4)`	Go to slide 4
`ActivePresentation.SlideShowWindow.View.Next`	Go to the next slide
`ActivePresentation.SlideShowWindow.View.Previous`	Go to the previous slide
`ActivePresentation.SlideShowWindow.View.First`	Go to the first slide
`ActivePresentation.SlideShowWindow.View.Last`	Go to the last slide
`ActivePresentation.SlideShowWindow.View.Exit`	Exit the slideshow

With the first statement, you can go to any slide in the presentation. Simply replace "3" with the number of any other slide. The only difficulty is that if you change the order of your slides, insert a new slide, or delete a slide, you will have to change the number. In Chapter 8, we will discuss naming slides. You will be able to set the names for your slides and use the name to go to a particular slide.

The ability to move around can be very powerful, particularly when the slide to which you want to go is based on something the user types or does. The next section reveals some secrets of MsgBox and ends with an example that moves to a particular slide based on which button is pressed in the MsgBox.

The Secrets of the MsgBox

Until now, we have used the MsgBox command to pop messages up on the screen. That is its main purpose. However, it can do more. Although it can't let the user type a message (use InputBox for that), MsgBox can display a few different combinations of buttons. If you don't tell it which buttons to use, it just has an OK button. The following table shows the different button combinations you can use along with the secret word, which we'll call a "constant," to access that combination. I'll explain the secret word after the table.

Button(s)	Constant
OK	vbOK
OK, Cancel	vbOKCancel
Abort, Retry, Ignore	vbAbortRetryIgnore
Yes, No, Cancel	vbYesNoCancel
Yes, No	vbYesNo
Retry, Cancel	vbRetryCancel

We can now use a MsgBox to ask a simple question. We don't have a lot of choices for the answers (just the limited choices above), but at least we can ask a yes/no question with a MsgBox. For anything more complicated, just use action buttons on a slide and skip the MsgBox.

To put more buttons in a MsgBox, we need to do two things: add a second argument to the MsgBox command (that's where the secret word comes in) and store the answer in a variable. Because the user can press one of two or three buttons, we need a way to keep track of which button was pressed. For example:

```
whichButton = MsgBox("Do you like chocolate?", vbYesNo)
```

The variable whichButton will store information about which button was pressed, and the second parameter to MsgBox (after the message that is to appear and the comma) is the constant that tells MsgBox which buttons to use. Figure 6.1 shows the MsgBox.

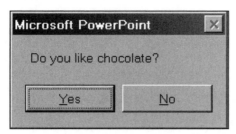

Figure 6.1. MsgBox with Yes and No Buttons

The secret words are called constants because they represent constant values (unlike variables, which can change value). In this case, the constants are mnemonics for numbers. For example, vbYesNo is really the number 4. Wherever you see the constant vbYesNo, you could type 4 instead. However, it might be easier to remember that vbYesNo means "I want Yes and No buttons" than remembering what 4 means in a MsgBox command. You can make your own constants, but we'll just use the ones that come with VBA; these usually start with the letters vb (for Visual Basic) or mso (for Microsoft Office), so if you ever see something that starts with vb or mso, it is probably a constant.

VBA comes with hundreds of constants that can be used with different commands, and it comes with a few more for the MsgBox command. The most important ones are values returned by MsgBox depending on which button was pressed. The following are the possible values: vbOK, vbCancel, vbAbort, vbRetry, vbIgnore, vbYes, and vbNo. For example, if the user clicks the Yes button, MsgBox returns vbYes. We might want to do something based on the button pressed. For example:

```
'Ask if you like chocolate. Give an appropriate response.
Sub Chocolate()
   Dim chocolateAnswer

   chocolateAnswer = MsgBox("Do you like chocolate?", vbYesNo)
   If chocolateAnswer = vbYes Then 'The user likes chocolate.
     MsgBox ("I like chocolate, too.")
   Else 'The user does not like chocolate.
     MsgBox ("Vanilla is a good choice.")
   End If
End Sub
```

Here is an example for a commonly used feature: a quit button. Sometimes users accidentally choose quit (by clicking on a button that calls a procedure with ActivePresentation.SlideShowWindow.View.Exit). To prevent quitting your presentation by accident, you might want to ask if the user really wants to quit. Associate the following procedure with your quit button:

```
'Ask if you are sure you want to quit. If the answer is Yes,
'exit the presentation. If the answer is No, go to the next slide.
Sub QuitOK()
    'result is a variable to keep track of which button is clicked.
    Dim result

    'MsgBox returns (will set the variable result to) vbYes if the
    'Yes button is clicked and vbNo if the No button is clicked.
    result = MsgBox("Are you sure you want to quit", vbYesNo)
    If result = vbYes Then 'Was the Yes button clicked?
        ActivePresentation.SlideShowWindow.View.Exit
    Else 'Since Yes wasn't clicked, it must be No
        ActivePresentation.SlideShowWindow.View.Next
    End If
End Sub
```

With the additional power of MsgBox, you have another tool to do something based on the answers to simple questions. By combining this with navigational commands from the previous section, you can let the user go anywhere in your presentation based on the answers to questions. But moving from slide to slide isn't the only response. You might want to stay on the same slide and have something magical happen. In the next section, you will learn how to make objects appear and disappear.

Hiding and Showing PowerPoint Objects

In PowerPoint, every object that you see on the screen (text boxes, buttons, pictures, etc.) has several properties that can be controlled by VBA. These might include the height and width of the object, the text displayed in the object, the color of the object, etc. Another property is whether or not the object is visible. If you want to be able to see the object, you can set its Visible property to True (note that VBA has a value that is msoTrue; this is the same as True for all your purposes, so don't worry if the VBA Editor suggests msoTrue; you can use msoTrue or True and it will work). If you want to hide the object, you set its Visible property to False (or msoFalse). For example, if you want to hide the fifth object on the second slide (see "Referencing Objects by Number" below if you don't know which is the fifth object), you could use the following line:

```
ActivePresentation.Slides(2).Shapes(5).Visible = False
```

Change False to True, and you show the object once again:

```
ActivePresentation.Slides(2).Shapes(5).Visible = True
```

For example, you might want a star to appear on a slide when a user gets the correct answer. To do this, create the star where you want it (using regular PowerPoint drawing tools). Even add text, such as "Good job!" See "Manipulating Text in Objects" below for more about changing the text on the fly to include the current score or the user's name. Before this can work effectively, we'll need to set up the presentation before the user gets to the slide with the star. This will require us to initialize the presentation.

Let's Get Started: Initializing Your Presentation

Up to this point, the user could go to any slide and not worry how it looked or even what was in any of the variables except possibly userName. As our presentations get more complicated, we will need to keep track of many different things. It will be important that everything in the presentation starts out how you want it. You don't want the user to go to a slide that has a star before choosing the right answer that is supposed to show the star. If you're keeping score, you want to be sure that the score starts at 0.

These kinds of things should be set up at the beginning of the presentation. One of the best ways to do this is with a button on the title slide. If it is the only button on that slide and you are in Kiosk mode, you know the user has to click that button to continue. All that the user might see is that the button goes to the next slide or asks for a name, but behind the scenes, your procedure is cleaning up everything (making the beds, dusting the furniture, setting up variables, hiding the toys and stars—all the things that you do before company comes).

In the hide and show example from the previous section, the one thing we want to do is hide our star. We will use a procedure called Initialize to do this (you could call it anything you want, like Housekeeper, Maid, or Mom). Let's imagine that you have two slides (slides 2 and 3) that will show stars when the correct answer is chosen. If the stars are the fourth object on the slides, your Initialize procedure might look something like this:

```
Sub Initialize()
    ActivePresentation.Slides(2).Shapes(4).Visible = False
    ActivePresentation.Slides(3).Shapes(4).Visible = False
End Sub
```

You could add something to this procedure to move to the next slide, or you can do all your initializing from this procedure and have another procedure take care of other stuff. So let's add a GetStarted procedure to do the other stuff as well as call the procedure Initialize.

```
Sub GetStarted()
    Initialize 'Hide the stars
    YourName 'Ask for the name
    ActivePresentation.SlideShowWindow.View.Next 'Go to the next slide
End Sub
```

This procedure will be linked to the button on the title slide. As the comments indicate, it will use the Initialize procedure to hide the stars, it will use the YourName procedure to ask for a name, and it will use ActivePresentation.SlideShowWindow.View.Next to go to the next slide. As always, because this procedure calls the YourName procedure and the Initialize procedure, these procedures must be included in your module along with the declaration (Dim statement) for the userName variable.

As you keep track of more things, you will set up more things in the `Initialize` procedure. This will include more objects that might be hidden or shown and variables, like ones to store the number of correct and incorrect answers that need to be given initial values. You'll see more about this in Chapter 7 when we start keeping score.

Finally, tying this all together, slides 2 and 3 will need buttons to show the stars. These buttons might be the right answer buttons on those slides. For example, the right answer on slide 2 might be linked to

```
Sub RightAnswerTwo
    ActivePresentation.Slides(2).Shapes(4).Visible = True
End Sub
```

Other things could happen in the `RightAnswerTwo` procedure, such as adding one to the number of correct answers or putting up a `MsgBox`, but until we get to Chapter 7, a star with the text "Good job" will be enough.

Figure 6.2 shows the VBA script and slides for this example. The arrows show which button should be connected to which procedure. The stars are showing in the figure, but they will be hidden in the `GetStarted` procedure and shown when the correct answer is chosen.

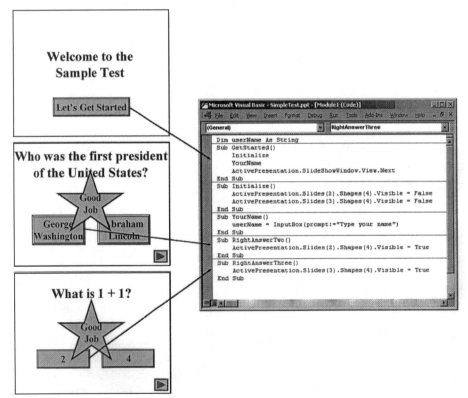

Figure 6.2. Simple Quiz Showing Stars for Correct Answers

Referencing Objects by Number

In the above example, we hid and showed shape number 4 on slide number 2. You might be asking, "How do I know what the shape number is? I want to hide that star, and I don't know what number it is." The number of an object generally is the order in which it was added to a slide. If you start with a blank slide and add a text box, a rectangle, and a button (in that order), the text box will be shape number 1, the rectangle will be shape number 2, and the button will be shape number 3. If you start with a slide that is not blank, the existing shapes will count. So, if you start with a bulleted list slide (known as a "Title and Text" slide in PowerPoint 2002) and add the text box, rectangle, and button,

- the slide title will be shape number 1,
- the bulleted list text area will be shape number 2,
- the text box you added will be shape number 3,
- the rectangle will be shape number 4, and
- the button will be shape number 5.

This is fine, but most of us don't have superhuman memories that can remember what order shapes were added. For PowerPoint versions 97, 98, 2000, and 2001, finding the number is easy. While looking at a slide, go to the Slide Show menu and choose "Custom Animation." Click on the "Timing" or "Order & Timing" tab, as shown in Figure 6.3.

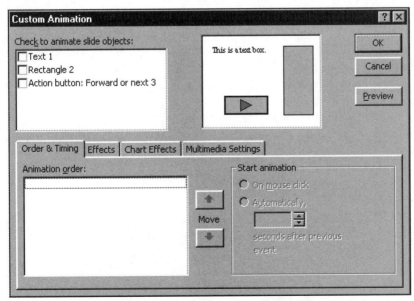

Figure 6.3. Custom Animation to Find Shape Numbers

In the upper left corner of the dialog box, you will see the objects listed by type and number. You can see that the text object is shape 1, the rectangle is shape 2, and the action button is shape 3. If you have lots of objects of the same type, you can click on the type and number of an object and the object will be highlighted on the right.

Once you have figured out the number of the object you want, you can close the dialog box with or without setting any animation.

For PowerPoint 2002, Custom Animation does not list all the objects on the slide, but it will list the objects that are animated. Therefore, if you want to find out an object's number, click on the object to select it, choose "Custom Animation" from the Slide Show menu, and add an animation effect (see Figure 6.4). Just as in earlier versions of PowerPoint, the number that appears after the object type is the object's number. In this case, the rectangle was selected, and it is object number 2 because the animation list shows "Rectangle 2." Note that the number 1 on the slide and in the animation list refers to the animation order, not the object number. After determining the object's number, don't forget to remove the animation effect by clicking on the "Remove" button in the "Custom Animation" window.

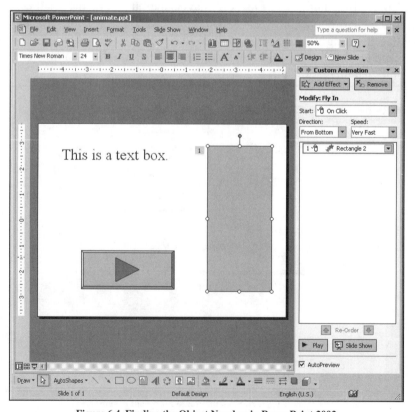

Figure 6.4. Finding the Object Number in PowerPoint 2002

The difficulty with referencing objects by number is that numbers change. This can happen if you delete an object from your slide or change the drawing order of your objects (by going to the Draw menu and choosing something from the Order submenu). When you delete an object from a slide, all the higher numbered objects change. For example, in our slide above with the text object, the rectangle, and the button, if we delete the text object, the rectangle becomes object number 1, and the button becomes object number 2. If you had written a script to do something to the rectangle, referencing the rectangle as object 2, your script would not work. That is why it is better to reference objects by name; names do not change unless you change them.

Referencing Objects by Name

Every object on a slide has a name. Anything you can do with an object's number, you can do with its name. Names are better than numbers because names of objects don't change unless you change them. The bad news is that there is no easy way (in any version of PowerPoint) to get the name of an object. Using VBA to determine the name of an object or change the name of an object is described in Chapter 8.

There is some logic to the names that are given to objects, so you might be able to figure out the name of an object. Each object's name starts with the type of object followed by a number. The main types of objects are Text Box, Rectangle, Line, Oval, Picture, and AutoShape. If the object isn't one of the other types, it is probably AutoShape. The numbers are assigned in order as the shapes are added to the slide, except that the numbering always starts with 2. Therefore, if you add a text object, a rectangle, and button to a blank slide, the objects will be named Text Box 2, Rectangle 3, and AutoShape 4 (see Figure 6.5). If there are already objects on the slide, the numbers will start higher. For example, if you add the same shapes to a bulleted list slide, the slide already contains Rectangle 2 (the title area) and Rectangle 3 (the bulleted list area), so your added shapes will be Text Box 4, Rectangle 5, and AutoShape 6.

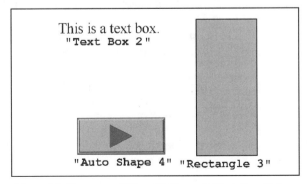

Figure 6.5. Shapes on a Slide, with Names in Quotations Below

These names do not change unless you change them. If you delete Text Box 4, Rectangle 5 and AutoShape 6 will keep the same name, and nothing will have a name with 4 in it. The number added to new names keeps going up even when you delete shapes. Thus, if you add the above shapes and then delete them and then insert a picture from clip art, the picture will be named Picture 7 even though no objects include 4, 5, and 6 in their names.

In order to use the name of an object, use it in quotes in the same place you would use the object number. Thus, to hide a shape named Text Box 4 on slide number 5, you could use the following line:

```
ActivePresentation.Slides(5).Shapes("Text Box 4").Visible = False
```

Of course, remembering shape names is just as hard as remembering shape numbers. Check out the scripts in Chapter 8 that will let you make up your own shape names.

This Slide or Another Slide

In the above examples, our scripts to hide and show objects specified which slides contained the objects. Sometimes you want an action to affect the current slide without regard to which number slide it is. For example, you might want to show an object on the current slide or add some text to a text box on the current slide or change the color of a menu item on the current slide. This is particularly useful when you want to write one procedure that will work on several slides. For example, if our DoingWell procedure revealed a star and each slide had a star with the same name or number, we could add a line to DoingWell to show the star on the current slide. One DoingWell procedure would be used for all the slides.

Sometimes you might want an action to affect another slide. You might be on one slide but wish to have something change on another slide, as we saw in our Initialize procedure. In the Initialize example, we wanted the slide to be set up properly before the user got there, so the change happened to the other slides when the user was on the first slide. We also want changes to happen before we arrive at a slide. If we hide our star (or change text on a slide or change the color of menu items) just as we arrive at a slide, the hidden object will be on the screen for a split second before disappearing. In some cases, this might not be a big problem, but if the action is to hide the answer to the question, this could be very important.

Anything affecting the current slide will start with

```
ActivePresentation.SlideShowWindow.View.Slide
```

So, for example, if you want to hide shape number 7 on the current slide, you would use this line:

```
ActivePresentation.SlideShowWindow.View.Slide.Shapes(7).Visible = False
```

Anything affecting another slide will start with

```
ActivePresentation.Slides(NUM)
```

where NUM is replaced by the number of the slide. So, for example, if you want to hide shape number 7 on slide number 2, you would use this line:

```
ActivePresentation.Slides(2).Shapes(7).Visible = False
```

Any expression throughout this book that uses a statement to affect the current slide can be changed to use a statement for another slide, and any expression that uses a statement to affect another slide can be changed to use a statement for the current slide.

Adding PowerPoint Objects

In the previous sections, we hid and showed any objects that we wanted after using normal PowerPoint drawing features to create the objects. Any object that you can create with PowerPoint drawing tools you can create and manipulate with VBA. In fact, you could use VBA to create your entire presentation, including all the slides, all the buttons, all the shapes, and all the text. For almost all your purposes, you are better off creating the shapes with PowerPoint drawing tools and using VBA to hide and show them, but in Chapters 7 and 10, we'll see examples that create slides and add shapes to them using VBA.

The problem with adding shapes is that they can collect in your presentation and can be hard for you to delete. For example, consider the star we hid and showed earlier in this chapter. Instead of hiding it and showing it, we could use VBA to create it. The problem is that once the shape is created, it is part of the presentation. Unless you are careful, you will have that shape (and possibly several copies of that shape) incorporated into your presentation. You can delete the shape when you are done, but this is an extra thing to track and not generally worth the effort.

If you are not dissuaded from adding shapes and would like to try it, you can try this example. If you heed my warnings, you'll skip this, go on to the next section, and only come back to this to understand the examples in Chapters 7 and 10.

Let's add a simple square in the middle of the screen:

```
Sub AddRectangle()
    Dim myShape As Shape

    Set myShape = _
        ActivePresentation.SlideShowWindow.View.Slide.Shapes. _
        AddShape(Type:=msoShapeRectangle, Left:=100, Top:=100, _
        Width:=200, Height:=200)
    myShape.Fill.ForeColor.RGB = vbRed
    myShape.TextFrame.TextRange.Text = "Hello"
End Sub
```

This looks complicated, but it is not as complicated as it looks. This procedure does three things: It creates the rectangle, it turns it red, and it puts the word "Hello" inside. Let's take it line by line:

```
Dim myShape As Shape
```

We are going to create a shape, so we create a variable to hold that shape. That way, once the shape is created, we can refer to it later in the procedure. Next we create the shape:

```
Set myShape = _
    ActivePresentation.SlideShowWindow.View.Slide.Shapes. _
    AddShape(Type:=msoShapeRectangle, Left:=100, Top:=100, _
    Width:=200, Height:=200)
```

`ActivePresentation.SlideShowWindow.View.Slide` gives us the current slide. `Shapes` gives us the shapes on the slide, and the `AddShape` method is used to add a shape to the shapes on the slide. Now, everything between the parentheses is simply telling you about the shape:

- The `Type` is what shape you are creating: `msoShapeRectangle` for a rectangle.

- `Left` and `Top` are the location on the screen of the top left corner of the shape

- `Width` and `Height` are how wide and tall the shape is.

Some other shapes you might use instead of `msoShapeRectangle` are:

msoShape4pointStar	msoShapeIsoscelesTriangle
msoShape5pointStar	msoShapeLeftArrow
msoShape8pointStar	msoShapeLightningBolt
msoShapeBalloon	msoShapeMoon
msoShapeBentArrow	msoShapeNoSymbol
msoShapeBentUpArrow	msoShapeOctagon
msoShapeCross	msoShapeOval
msoShapeCube	msoShapeParallelogram
msoShapeCurvedDownArrow	msoShapePentagon
msoShapeCurvedLeftArrow	msoShapeRectangle
msoShapeCurvedRightArrow	msoShapeRightArrow
msoShapeCurvedUpArrow	msoShapeRightTriangle
msoShapeDiamond	msoShapeRoundedRectangle
msoShapeDonut	msoShapeSmileyFace
msoShapeDownArrow	msoShapeSun
msoShapeHeart	msoShapeTrapezoid
msoShapeHexagon	msoShapeUpArrow

Try replacing `msoShapeRectangle` with some of the other shapes from this list.

Finally, we set some properties of the shape. Since the shape is stored in the variable `myShape`, we can use `myShape` to manipulate some of the shape's properties:

```
myShape.Fill.ForeColor.RGB = vbRed
```

This line takes the shape we just created and stored in the variable `myShape` and adjusts its color. This looks complicated, but you just have to remember that if you want to change the color of a shape, you need to adjust the `.Fill.ForeColor.RGB`. After the equal sign is the color we want. There are many ways to specify the exact color, but you can use the following basic colors: `vbBlack`, `vbRed`, `vbGreen`, `vbYellow`, `vbBlue`, `vbMagenta`, `vbCyan`, and `vbWhite`.

Shapes can also have words in them. If you want to set the text in the shape to "Hello," use the following line:

```
myShape.TextFrame.TextRange.Text = "Hello"
```

This is simply a long way of saying that the text in this shape should be set to "Hello."

Adding objects can be useful, especially if you want the user to make significant changes to the presentation. In the example in Chapter 10, the user adds slides to the presentation. These slides become part of the presentation, and there are an undetermined number of them (every user that goes through the presentation can add slides to it). In most cases, however, you will have a few shapes that you have determined in advance. Rather than creating those shapes in VBA, you would do better to create them in PowerPoint and hide and show them with VBA. This will prevent your presentation from getting cluttered with extra shapes when a user hits a button too many times and adds several extra shapes.

Putting the Student's Input into a Box

When we created a shape ourselves, we could easily add text to it. Since the variable `myShape` pointed to the shape, we were able to use `myShape` to change any of the shape's properties, including the text in the shape. We can do the same thing with a shape that we created with PowerPoint's drawing tools.

```
ActivePresentation.SlideShowWindow.View.Slide.Shapes(3)
```

refers to the third shape on the current slide, so

```
ActivePresentation.SlideShowWindow.View.Slide.Shapes(3) _
    .TextFrame.TextRange.Text
```

refers to the text on the third shape of the current slide.

```
ActivePresentation.SlideShowWindow.View.Slide.Shapes(3) _
    .TextFrame.TextRange.Text = "Hello"
```

changes the text of the third shape of the current slide to "Hello."

Now, we can put this together with YourName and Initialize to put the user's name in the text box:

```
Dim userName

'Link this to the first button on the title slide.
Sub GetStarted()
    Initialize 'Hide the stars
    YourName 'Ask for the name
    ActivePresentation.SlideShowWindow.View.Next 'Go to the next slide
End Sub

'GetStarted calls this so no buttons link to this directly.
'This assumes that slides 2 and 3 will have the 4th shape that
'you will want to show when the right answer is chosen.
Sub Initialize()
    ActivePresentation.Slides(2).Shapes(4).Visible = False
    ActivePresentation.Slides(3).Shapes(4).Visible = False
End Sub

'GetStarted calls this to ask for a name.
Sub YourName()
    Dim done As Boolean

    done = False
    While Not done
        userName = InputBox(prompt:="Type your name", _
            Title:="Input Name")
        If userName = "" Then
            done = False
        Else
            done = True
        End If
    Wend
End Sub

'Link this to the button that contains the right answer on each slide.
'Be sure you have used your drawing tools to create the 4th shape
'on each slide.
'Note that this RightAnswer does not automatically go to the next
'slide.
Sub RightAnswer
    ActivePresentation.SlideShowWindow.View.Slide.Shapes(4) _
        .TextFrame.TextRange.Text = "Good job, " & userName
    ActivePresentation.SlideShowWindow.View.Slide.Shapes(4).Visible = True
End Sub
```

You have seen most of this before. GetStarted, Initialize, and YourName are just like what we used earlier. The only new thing is in RightAnswer. Rather than using a simple string, like "Hello," for the text in the object, we put together some text with the user's name, just like we did with a `MsgBox` in our earlier `DoingWell` procedures.

Of course, you can do the same thing with a shape that you use VBA to create, but you can figure that out for yourself.

Manipulating Text in Objects

In the previous section, we changed the text in a shape by accessing the shape's `.TextFrame.TextRange.Text`. Now that you have access to that part of a shape, you can do whatever you want to the text in that shape. This is useful for changing the text in shapes you draw with the drawing tools, in shapes you create with VBA with `AddShape`, and in shapes that come with PowerPoint slides (such as the title or bulleted text area on a slide). But you can do more than simply change the text on a shape to something new. You can manipulate the text in many different ways. This section doesn't cover all of them, but it is enough to get you started exploring.

`With` Blocks

Before changing the text, we should learn a simple VBA trick to save you from typing long expressions over and over again. You might have noticed that to get to the text for a shape, you have to type something very long, such as

```
ActivePresentation.SlideShowWindow.View.Slide.Shapes(3).TextFrame _
    .TextRange.Text
```

This refers to the text in the third shape in the current slide (it's interesting how I can say it in English in less space than I can say it in VBA). To save typing, we can use a `With` block. For example, if we want to do several things to the third shape on the current slide, we can do the following:

```
With ActivePresentation.SlideShowWindow.View.Slide.Shapes(3)
    .TextFrame.TextRange.Text = "Hello"
    .Fill.ForeColor.RGB = vbRed
    .Visible = True
End With
```

The `With` block (starting with the first line that begins with `With` and ending with the line that ends with `End With`) simply assumes that anything starting with a dot really includes all the stuff on the `With` line. In English, it is saying, "I want to do the following things to the third shape on the current slide: change the text to 'Hello', change the background color to red, and make the shape visible."

Adding Text

Now, suppose you want to add something to the text in your shape, rather than replace the text. Remember the ampersand (&). This is used to join two pieces of text together. We used it when we wanted to display text in a MsgBox that included "You are doing well" and the user's name. We can use it here to join what is already in the text box with some additional text. Once we join together the text we need to stick the joined together text into the .Text of the shape.

```
Sub AddHello()
   With ActivePresentation.SlideShowWindow.View.Slide _
      .Shapes("Rectangle 3")
      .TextFrame.TextRange.Text = _
         .TextFrame.TextRange.Text & Chr$(13) & "Hello Mother"
   End With
End Sub
```

The With line (including the next line that is really part of that line due to the underscore) tells the computer that we are going to do something with the shape named "Rectangle 3" on the current slide. If the current slide is a Bulleted List slide, "Rectangle 3" refers to the bulleted list area (the main area for text).

```
.TextFrame.TextRange.Text = _
```

tells the computer that we are going to put something into the text area of that slide. After the equal sign, the next line

```
.TextFrame.TextRange.Text & Chr$(13) & "Hello Mother"
```

tells the computer what we are going to put into the text area. We are going to

- start with what is already there (.TextFrame.TextRange.Text);
- add to that a special character, Chr$(13), which is the New Paragraph symbol (just like hitting "Enter" or "Return" if you were typing the text into the text area yourself); and
- add the text "Hello Mother".

This will have the effect of taking what was already in the bulleted list and adding a new line with the words "Hello Mother." Remember, you can do anything with the text that you want. We added "Hello Mother" as a simple example. You could have added the user's name. For example, you might write an interactive story with your students in which the student types a name at the beginning of the story, and the name is used during the story by replacing or modifying the text in one of the slides:

```
Sub BrickPig()
   With ActivePresentation.Slides(7).Shapes("Rectangle 3")
      .TextFrame.TextRange.Text = .TextFrame.TextRange.Text & _
      "And then the third pig, " & userName & _
      ", built a house of bricks. The brick house " & _
      "was very strong."
   End With
End Sub
```

This takes the shape named "Rectangle 3" on the seventh slide and adds text to it that includes the user's name (assuming you have used the YourName procedure at some previous point to get the user's name). If "Rectangle 3" is a Placeholder (see below for information about Placeholders), be sure it has something in it when you try to run this code, or your text will not show up until after you exit Slide Show View.

As another example, imagine that you are having a class discussion, and you want to record the students' comments in your PowerPoint presentation. Perhaps you are discussing the signs of spring, and you want the class to tell you signs of spring related to plants and animals. Without technology, you would write the information on the blackboard. However, this is awkward if you are using PowerPoint as part of the discussion; it is awkward to run from the computer to the blackboard, and it is awkward to flip the lights off and on so students can see the screen and the blackboard alternately. Instead, use this simple code to put the text right into the PowerPoint presentation:

```
Sub AddPlants()
   Dim newstuff As String

   newstuff = InputBox("What is a plant sign of Spring?")
   If newstuff  "" Then
      With ActivePresentation.SlideShowWindow.View.Slide _
         .Shapes(2).TextFrame.TextRange
         .Text = .Text + Chr$(13) + newstuff
      End With
   End If
End Sub

Sub AddAnimals()
   Dim newstuff As String

   newstuff = InputBox("What is an animal sign of Spring?")
   If newstuff  "" Then
      With ActivePresentation.SlideShowWindow.View.Slide. _
         Shapes(3).TextFrame.TextRange
         .Text = .Text + Chr$(13) + newstuff
      End With
   End If
End Sub
```

This code works on a slide with two text boxes that you add as the second and third shapes on the slide, and it works with a 2-Column Text slide. Just beware that if you add text to an empty Placeholder (that's one of those text boxes that says "Click to add text" or "Click to add title" before you put anything in it, i.e., your title, left column, and right column in the 2-Column Text slide), your text will not show up until you exit the slideshow. To avoid this problem, either use a Title Only slide and draw your own text boxes or type a space in the text area so the Placeholder is not empty.

The code works with the slide shown in Figure 6.6. This figure shows the slide before and after typing some text. In this case, you would have pressed the Plant button (which is tied to the `AddPlant` procedure) twice and the Animal button (which is tied to the `AddAnimal` procedure) once, having been prompted by an `InputBox` each time to name a sign of spring. The `If` statement in each procedure (along with the corresponding `End If`) can be left off, but it provides you with an escape if you accidentally hit the wrong button: Simply click OK without typing anything. The `If` statement asks if you have typed something (i.e., the text you typed is not the empty string), and it only adds the text to the slide if the answer is yes.

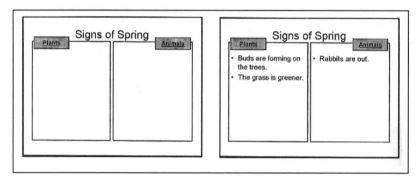

Figure 6.6. Signs of Spring Discussion Slide—Before and After

Of course the entire example could be simplified with one procedure, one text box, and one button if you don't want to organize student responses into two columns. It can also be complicated by adding more similar procedures, more text boxes, and more buttons if you want to divide student responses into more than two areas.

Manipulating Parts of Text in an Object

`TextRange` is an interesting creature. The `TextRange` of a shape refers to the entire text in that shape, but anything you can do to a `TextRange`, you can do to a part of a `TextRange`. You can do things to specific paragraphs within the `TextRange`, specific words within the `TextRange`, and specific characters within the `TextRange`.

For example, if you wanted to change to blue the color of the text in the entire third shape of the current slide, you could use the following code:

```
ActivePresentation.SlideShowWindow.View.Slide.Shapes(3). _
    TextFrame.TextRange.Font.Color.RGB = vbBlue
```

Almost identical code can be used to change the second *paragraph* of the third shape on the current slide to blue:

```
ActivePresentation.SlideShowWindow.View.Slide.Shapes(3). _
   TextFrame.TextRange.Paragraphs(2).Font.Color.RGB = vbBlue
```

Note that paragraphs include the New Paragraph symbol, Chr$(13), as part of the paragraph. Thus, you must be careful when changing the text of a paragraph to be sure that each paragraph ends with Chr$(13). See the Mystery Example later in this chapter for an example of this. With another small change, the second *word* becomes blue:

```
ActivePresentation.SlideShowWindow.View.Slide.Shapes(3). _
   TextFrame.TextRange.Words(2).Font.Color.RGB = vbBlue
```

Note that VBA counts punctuation marks as words. For example, the text "Hello, my name is David" has six words (by VBA's count; who said computers were smart?), with the comma being the second word. With another small change, the second *character* becomes blue:

```
ActivePresentation.SlideShowWindow.View.Slide.Shapes(3). _
   TextFrame.TextRange.Characters(2).Font.Color.RGB = vbBlue
```

Finally, any of these statements can be altered slightly to include a range of paragraphs, words, or characters. Simply include a second number after the "2" to tell how many paragraphs, words, or characters you want to affect. For example, if you want to make seven characters blue, starting with the second one, you would use the following:

```
ActivePresentation.SlideShowWindow.View.Slide.Shapes(3). _
   TextFrame.TextRange.Characters(2,7).Font.Color.RGB = vbBlue
```

If the text is "Hello, mother," then the characters "ello, m" would turn blue (the comma and space count as the fifth and sixth characters).

What Can You Change?

All of the examples above changed the color of the text using .Font.Color.RGB. This is one of many things that you can change about the font of the text. You can change Bold, Italic, Shadow, and Underline to True or False. For example:

```
ActivePresentation.SlideShowWindow.View.Slide.Shapes(3). _
   TextFrame.TextRange.Font.Bold = True
```

This is the same as if you had selected the text and clicked on the Bold button in the toolbar.

You can also set the `Size` of the text to a particular point size. For example, if you wanted to change the text to a 12-point font size, you could use the following:

```
ActivePresentation.SlideShowWindow.View.Slide.Shapes(3). _
   TextFrame.TextRange.Font.Size = 12
```

You can change the `Name` of the font, but you should beware; if this presentation is running on a variety of computers, you should stay away from fonts that are not standard because your font will only show up properly if the computer on which the presentation is running has the font. To change the font to Helvetica, you can use the following example:

```
ActivePresentation.SlideShowWindow.View.Slide.Shapes(3). _
   TextFrame.TextRange.Font.Name = "Helvetica"
```

Finally, you can change the color in a number of ways. You have already seen that you can choose from some VBA constant colors: `vbBlack`, `vbRed`, `vbGreen`, `vbYellow`, `vbBlue`, `vbMagenta`, `vbCyan`, and `vbWhite`. You can also set colors by using an RGB value. RGB stands for Red Green Blue. You will specify a color by indicating how much red, how much green, and how much blue the color contains. For example, to make the text red, you could use the following:

```
ActivePresentation.SlideShowWindow.View.Slide.Shapes(3). _
   TextFrame.TextRange.Font.Color.RGB = RGB(255,0,0)
```

This means that you want lots of red, no green, and no blue (the numbers range from 0 to 255). You can experiment with the numbers to find just the right shade you want. For example, `RGB(150,0,75)` gives a lovely shade of purple.

Other Things You Can Do to Text

Many things that traditional PowerPoint can do to text, VBA can do as well. If you want to make changes while creating a presentation, using PowerPoint's menus to do things is probably easiest. VBA is useful when you want to change things in response to something the user does. You can use VBA to `Cut`, `Copy`, `Delete`, or `Paste` text:

```
ActivePresentation.SlideShowWindow.View.Slide.Shapes(3). _
   .TextFrame.TextRange.Words(3,2).Cut
ActivePresentation.SlideShowWindow.View.Slide.Shapes(3). _
   .TextFrame.TextRange.Words(4,2).Paste
```

This will cut the third and fourth words in the third shape of the current slide (remember the "3,2" means start with the third word and do this for two words). Next it will find the fourth and fifth words (counting words without the text that was just cut) and replace them with what you cut. So if the text was "one two three four five six seven eight nine ten," the `Cut` will change the text to "one two five six seven eight nine ten," and the `Paste` will change it to "one two five three four eight nine ten." Change the `Cut` to `Delete` to get rid of the text without the ability to paste it, and change it to `Copy` to copy the text without removing it from the original location.

You can also find out how long (i.e., how many characters) a `TextRange` is with `Length`:

```
MsgBox (ActivePresentation.SlideShowWindow.View.Slide.Shapes(3). _
    .TextFrame.TextRange.Length)
```

This will pop up a `MsgBox` with the number of characters in the third shape of the current slide.

Finally, you might want to know how many words or paragraphs are in a `TextRange`. You can use `Count` to find this out:

```
MsgBox (ActivePresentation.SlideShowWindow.View.Slide.Shapes(3). _
    .TextFrame.TextRange.Paragraphs.Count)
```

This will pop up a `MsgBox` with the number of paragraphs (change `Paragraphs` to `Words` to get the number of words).

Manipulating Text: The Mystery Example

You have seen many tricks for manipulating text, but you might be wondering how they might fit into a real example. This section includes a simple example of a presentation that solves a mystery. This is a simple mystery with only two clues, but you should be able to expand it to include more clues. Figure 6.7 (page 86) shows the slides in this mystery. Figure 6.8 (page 87) shows the VBA code for the presentation.

In this simple example, most of the navigation is done with traditional PowerPoint buttons. The forward and back arrows are linked to the next and previous slides, the "Update Clue Sheet" button is linked to the last slide, and the "Return to Mystery" button is linked to the last slide viewed (i.e., if the user just came from Mystery Clue #1, it will go back to Mystery Clue #1).

The buttons that use VBA are on the first and last slides. The first slide has the "Let's Get Started" button that links to the `GetStarted` script. Although we don't have to initialize any variables, we do have to set up the last slide. This involves setting up the text area (which is the second shape) on the fifth slide with two paragraphs:

```
With ActivePresentation.Slides(5).Shapes(2).TextFrame.TextRange
    .Paragraphs(1).Text = "Eye Color:" & Chr$(13)
    .Paragraphs(2).Text = "Hair Color:"
End With
```

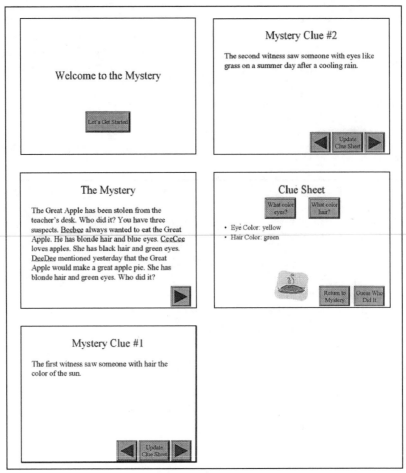

Figure 6.7. The Mystery Presentation Slides

This uses a `With` block because both paragraphs are part of the `TextRange` of the `TextFrame` of the second shape on the fifth slide. Note that we add `Chr$(13)`, the new paragraph symbol, to the end of the first paragraph. Without it, the paragraphs would run together.

We also want to hide the picture of the apple pie (which is the seventh shape on the fifth slide) because it will only be shown when the user gets the right answer:

```
ActivePresentation.Slides(5).Shapes(7).Visible = False
```

If you add more clues, update the `GetStarted` procedure to refer to whatever slide number is the last slide. That is, change the "5" to another number in both lines referring to the slide.

File   Edit   View   Insert   Format   Debug   Run   Tools   Add-Ins   Window   Help

(General)   (Declarations)

```vba
Dim userName As String
Dim userGuess As String
Dim userClue
Sub GetStarted()
    With ActivePresentation.Slides(5).Shapes(2).TextFrame.TextRange
        .Paragraphs(1).Text = "Eye Color:" & Chr$(13)
        .Paragraphs(2).Text = "Hair Color:"
    End With
    ActivePresentation.Slides(5).Shapes(7).Visible = False
    YourName
    ActivePresentation.SlideShowWindow.View.Next
End Sub
Sub YourName()
    userName = InputBox(prompt:="Type your name", _
        Title:="Input Name")
End Sub
Sub EyeColor()
    userClue = InputBox(prompt:="What is the eye color?")
    With ActivePresentation.Slides(5).Shapes(2).TextFrame.TextRange
        .Paragraphs(1).Text = "Eye Color: " & userClue & Chr$(13)
        If userClue = "blue" Then
            .Paragraphs(1).Words(4).Font.Color.RGB = vbBlue
        ElseIf userClue = "green" Then
            .Paragraphs(1).Words(4).Font.Color.RGB = vbGreen
        End If
    End With
End Sub
Sub HairColor()
    userClue = InputBox(prompt:="What is the hair color?")
    With ActivePresentation.Slides(5).Shapes(2).TextFrame.TextRange
        .Paragraphs(2).Text = "Hair Color: " & userClue
        If userClue = "blonde" Then
            .Paragraphs(2).Words(4).Font.Color.RGB = vbYellow
        ElseIf userClue = "black" Then
            .Paragraphs(2).Words(4).Font.Color.RGB = vbBlack
        End If
    End With
End Sub
Sub Guess()
    userGuess = InputBox(prompt:="Who did it?")
    If userGuess = "DeeDee" Then
        ActivePresentation.Slides(5).Shapes(7).Visible = True
        MsgBox ("You are right, " & userName & _
            ". Would you like a piece of pie?")
        ActivePresentation.SlideShowWindow.View.GotoSlide (1)
    ElseIf userGuess = "BeeBee" Then
        MsgBox ("Try again and check the eye color.")
    ElseIf userGuess = "CeeCee" Then
        MsgBox ("Try again and check the hair color.")
    Else
        MsgBox ("Try again")
    End If
End Sub
```

Figure 6.8. The Mystery Presentation VBA Code

EyeColor and HairColor are almost identical. The main difference is that EyeColor changes the text in the first paragraph and HairColor changes the text in the second paragraph. EyeColor uses an InputBox to prompt for the eye color and stores what the user types in the variable userClue. The With statement is just like the With in GetStarted, referring to the TextRange where the clues are stored. The code:

```
.Paragraphs(1).Text = "Eye Color: " & userClue & Chr$(13)
```

changes the first paragraph (the one that includes the eye color clue) to whatever the user typed. The If statement then checks to see if what was typed was "blue":

```
If userClue = "blue" Then
```

If it is, it changes the color of the fourth word (which would be the word "blue") to blue:

```
.Paragraphs(1).Words(4).Font.Color.RGB = vbBlue
```

The ElseIf part checks to see if the user typed green and changes the color of the text to green.

Guess uses an InputBox to ask for the user's guess. The part that checks for the correct answer is a series of If, ElseIf, ElseIf, ElseIf, and Else statements. The If section is for the right answer. It shows the picture of the apple pie (because DeeDee wanted the apple to make pie):

```
ActivePresentation.Slides(5).Shapes(7).Visible = True
```

It shows a MsgBox telling the user that the answer is correct:

```
MsgBox ("You are right, " & userName & _
    ". Would you like a piece of pie?")
```

And when the user clicks OK on the MsgBox, it jumps back to the beginning:

```
ActivePresentation.SlideShowWindow.View.GotoSlide (1)
```

The two ElseIf clauses each bring up a MsgBox with specific feedback about what was wrong, and the Else clause (if the user typed anything besides "DeeDee," "BeeBee," or "CeeCee") brings up a MsgBox that gives the generic feedback "Try again."

To create your own mystery, simply change text on the mystery and clue slides, change the text in the VBA code that refers specifically to eye color and hair color (in case your clues are about something else), change the text on the eye color and hair color buttons, and change the If block in the Guess procedure to give appropriate feedback for the possible guesses in your mystery. You might also want to change the picture of the apple pie to something else. If you add more clues, simply copy one of the clue slides, change the text, and change Slides(5) to Slides(6) or Slides(7) or whatever number the last slide is. Finally, you might have to adjust some of the shape numbers. For example, when you create this yourself, your picture (replacing the apple pie picture) might not be Shapes(7).

Conclusion

In this chapter you learned some powerful VBA tricks that allow you to move around in your presentation and manipulate the objects on your slides. You now have the power to hide and show objects and manipulate the text in your objects. This allows you to expand feedback from a simple MsgBox to something that changes the text in the slides. For simple feedback, a MsgBox is fine, but to incorporate what your students have to say into the fabric of the presentation, nothing beats changing the text on your slides. The discussion ended with a creative mystery example that shows how this technology can go beyond simple tutorials and quizzes. In the next chapter you will see how to build quizzes of varying complexity with different types of questions and different ways of tracking and reporting scores.

Exercises to Try

✍ Take the mystery example at the end of this chapter and rewrite it to include your own mystery. Start by changing the text of the mystery and updating the questions. Next, change the clue sheet to match your clues and change the apple pie picture to match your mystery.

✍ If you are feeling adventurous, try expanding the mystery beyond two clues by adding more clue slides and more paragraphs on the clue sheet.

7

Quizzes and Tests

Introduction

In Chapter 6 you learned a number of powerful tricks. In fact, you now have most of the basic skills you need to create a wide range of interactive projects. If you fancy yourself a programmer, you can stop here and figure everything else out for yourself. However, since this book is for scripters, we will continue with a few more tricks and many more examples.

In this chapter you will learn about different ways to create quizzes and tests with VBA. We'll start with simple multiple-choice tests, add scripts to keep score, give options for tests that only allow one try to get the right answer or allow multiple tries, add short-answer questions, add a script that creates a new slide with complete test results suitable for printing, and add a multiple-part tutorial that won't let your students take the test until they have completed the entire tutorial. By the time you finish this chapter, you will have the skills necessary to create tests in a variety of different ways.

Vocabulary

- `ActivePresentation.Slides.Add`
- `LCase`
- `numCorrect`
- `numIncorrect`
- `Round`
- `Trim`

Simple Multiple-Choice Tests

In Chapter 2 you learned about buttons and hyperlinks. This gave you the power to create a simple multiple-choice test with feedback. Without using VBA, you could create a text object and type the question in the text object. Below the text object, create buttons with possible answers. Link the button with the correct answer to a slide that has a text object that tells the student that the answer is correct. Link the buttons with the incorrect answers to a slide that has a text object that tells the student that the answer is incorrect. On the (correct and incorrect) feedback slides, create a button that leads to the next question, and repeat these steps for each question. This works, but it is a little bit cumbersome.

With a little bit of VBA from Chapter 4, you could eliminate the feedback slides and use a simple MsgBox for feedback, tying your buttons with right and wrong answers to the following procedures, respectively:

```
Sub RightAnswer()
   MsgBox ("Good job.")
End Sub

Sub WrongAnswer()
   MsgBox ("Try to do better.")
End Sub
```

With a little help from Chapter 5, you can include the user's name in your feedback:

```
Dim userName

Sub YourName()
   userName = InputBox(prompt:="What is your name?")
End Sub

Sub RightAnswer()
   MsgBox ("Good job, " & userName)
End Sub

Sub WrongAnswer()
   MsgBox ("Try to do better, " & userName)
End Sub
```

Next, add a little bit of help from Chapter 6 to automatically jump to the next question after the right answer is chosen:

```
Sub RightAnswer()
   MsgBox ("Good job, " & userName)
   ActivePresentation.SlideShowWindow.View.Next
End Sub
```

As usual, with a small amount of VBA, we have added a small amount of power: adding the user's name to the feedback and cutting down on the number of slides. These are small advantages over traditional PowerPoint. In the next section, we'll add more power by keeping score.

Keeping Score

If you create a test with the above procedures attached to the right and wrong answers, you don't have to change your slides or buttons at all to add scorekeeping; you just need some small additions to your VBA. Figure 7.1 shows the slides for a simple test along with the VBA code that gives feedback and keeps score. The arrows show which buttons are tied to which procedures.

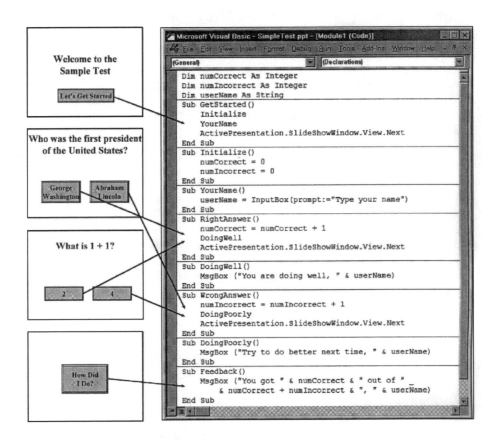

Figure 7.1. Multiple-Choice Test with Scorekeeping

Although this example only has two questions, and each question has two possible answers, this easily can be expanded to include more questions and more possible answers. In fact, the VBA script remains exactly the same. You simply add more slides and tie the buttons to the RightAnswer and WrongAnswer procedures.

In Chapter 6, we did something similar with GetStarted, Initialize, RightAnswer, and WrongAnswer, using stars for feedback and not keeping score. The significant additions to this script are the variables: numCorrect and numIncorrect. numCorrect contains the number of questions answered correctly. numIncorrect contains the number of questions answered incorrectly. Each time a correct answer is chosen, the procedure RightAnswer is called in which numCorrect is increased by one (numCorrect = numCorrect + 1). Each time a wrong answer is chosen, the procedure WrongAnswer is called in which numIncorrect is increased by one (numIncorrect = numIncorrect + 1). When you want to find out how you are doing, call the procedure Feedback to display a MsgBox with how many questions were right (numCorrect) out of how many were answered (numCorrect + numIncorrect). In addition, before the test starts, call the procedure GetStarted to initialize the variables (set numCorrect and numIncorrect to 0), ask for the student's name, and move to the first question. Other than the variables, all the parts of this script are things you have seen before.

You might want to report the score in other forms. Now that we know how many questions were answered correctly and how many were answered incorrectly, you can adjust the MsgBox command in the Feedback procedure to report in other ways. If you just want to report the number of right answers, try this:

```
MsgBox("You got " & numCorrect & "right, " & userName)
```

If you want to report the number of right answers and the number of wrong answers but not the total, you can use this:

```
MsgBox("You got " & numCorrect & " right and " _
    numIncorrect & " wrong, " & userName)
```

If you would like to report a percentage score, you can use this:

```
MsgBox ("You got " & _
    100 * numCorrect / (numIncorrect + numCorrect) & "%, " & userName)
```

Finally, if you want that percentage score rounded off, you can use this:

```
MsgBox ("You got " & _
    Round(100 * numCorrect / (numIncorrect + numCorrect), 0) & _
    "%, " & userName)
```

Note that the 0 represents how many places after the decimal point to show, so if you like the result "33%," use 0; if you like the result "33.3%," use 1; etc.

This is just the tip of the iceberg with what you can do with tests. Variables can be used to keep track of any information you want; for example, you could allow students to try answering a question again but only count the first try.

More complicated scripts can be used to judge other kinds of test questions; short-answer questions are a small step away. With VBA, the possibilities are endless.

Try Again: Answer Until It's Right

Keeping score is easy when you only get one chance to answer each question. What if you want your students to answer the questions until they get them right? How difficult this is depends on how you want to keep score. If you want to count every attempt, you don't have to change much. Simply delete `ActivePresentation.SlideShowWindow.View.Next` from the `WrongAnswer` procedure. This will stop the presentation from going to the next question after a wrong answer, but it will count every click on the wrong answer as well as the click on the right answer. For example, if you use the questions from Figure 7.1 (page 93) and click on Abraham Lincoln (the wrong answer for question 1), then George Washington (the right answer for question 1), then 2 (the right answer for question 2), your score will be two out of three because you got the first question wrong once then right once, and you got the second question right once.

If you want to count only the first try, in the above example you would want a score of one out of two. That is because you got the first question wrong on the first try, and you got the second question right on the first try. This requires no changes to your slides, including which buttons are tied to which procedures. It only requires the following code; changes from the code in Figure 7.1 are marked with comments (`'ADDED` for additions and `'DELETED` for the line that is deleted):

```
Dim numCorrect As Integer
Dim numIncorrect As Integer
Dim userName As String
Dim qAnswered As Boolean 'ADDED

Sub GetStarted()
   Initialize
   YourName
   ActivePresentation.SlideShowWindow.View.Next
End Sub

Sub Initialize()
   numCorrect = 0
   numIncorrect = 0
   qAnswered = False 'ADDED
End Sub

Sub YourName()
   userName = InputBox(prompt:="Type your name")
End Sub
```

```
Sub RightAnswer()
    If qAnswered = False Then 'ADDED
        numCorrect = numCorrect + 1
    End If 'ADDED
    qAnswered = False 'ADDED
    DoingWell
    ActivePresentation.SlideShowWindow.View.Next
End Sub

Sub DoingWell()
    MsgBox ("You are doing well, " & userName)
End Sub

Sub WrongAnswer()
    If qAnswered = False Then 'ADDED
        numIncorrect = numIncorrect + 1
    End If 'ADDED
    qAnswered = True 'ADDED
    DoingPoorly
    'DELETED ActivePresentation.SlideShowWindow.View.Next
End Sub

Sub DoingPoorly()
    MsgBox ("Try to do better next time, " & userName)
End Sub

Sub Feedback()
    MsgBox ("You got " & numCorrect & " out of " _
        & numCorrect + numIncorrect & ", " & userName)
End Sub
```

The heart of this procedure is the variable qAnswered. It keeps track of whether or not the current question has been answered yet. If it is False, the question has not yet been answered; if it is True, the question has been answered.

A small amount of code is added to the Dim section to declare qAnswered so that all the procedures know about it. It also must be initialized to False in the Initialize procedure so it is False when you get to the first question. Finally, RightAnswer and WrongAnswer must check and adjust the value of qAnswered.

RightAnswer and WrongAnswer check to see if the question has not been answered yet If (qAnswered = False) Then and only add one to numCorrect or numIncorrect if qAnswered is False; that is, the question has not yet been answered. In addition RightAnswer sets qAnswered to False before going to the next question, and WrongAnswer sets qAnswered to True before letting you try again (by not going to the next question).

Try Again and Again: Answer Again After It's Right

The previous example works fine as long as your students are forced to move to the next question (and can't come back) once they have gotten the right answer. This gets more complicated if you allow students to come back to questions later. The problem is that we need to keep track of more things; that is, we need variables to remember if each question has been answered: `q1Answered`, `q2Answered`, etc. As you begin to understand this example, you might think of other things that you want to remember. In a later example in this chapter, we will keep track of not only which questions have been answered but also what those answers were. If you want to try to go beyond the examples in this book, remember that you can create as many variables as you want to keep track of as many things as you want.

To allow students to revisit questions as many times as they want, you will have to alter your question slides to include buttons that move to the next and previous slides, as in Figure 7.2.

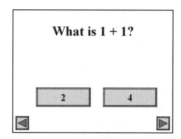

Figure 7.2. Question Slide with Next and Previous Buttons

The other change to your slides will be to tie your right and wrong answer buttons to new procedures. We will need a new procedure for each question's right and wrong answers, rather than one procedure for all right answers and one for all wrong answers. These specialized procedures will check the variables (`q1Answered`, `q2Answered`, . . .) to see if the questions have been answered and will update the variables and the score appropriately.

Here is the complete VBA code for this example. Comments have been used to indicate changes from the previous example:

```
Dim numCorrect As Integer
Dim numIncorrect As Integer
Dim userName As String
Dim q1Answered As Boolean 'ADDED to replace qAnswered
Dim q2Answered As Boolean 'ADDED to replace qAnswered

Sub GetStarted()
   Initialize
   YourName
   ActivePresentation.SlideShowWindow.View.Next
End Sub

Sub Initialize()
   numCorrect = 0
   numIncorrect = 0
   q1Answered = False 'ADDED to replace qAnswered
   q2Answered = False 'ADDED to replace qAnswered
End Sub
```

```
Sub YourName()
   userName = InputBox(prompt:="Type your name")
End Sub

Sub RightAnswer1() 'ADDED to replace RightAnswer
   If q1Answered = False Then
      numCorrect = numCorrect + 1
   End If
   q1Answered = True 'Do not reset q1Answered to FALSE
   DoingWell
   'DELETED ActivePresentation.SlideShowWindow.View.Next
End Sub

Sub RightAnswer2() 'Same as RightAnswer1 with 1 changed to 2
   If q2Answered = False Then
      numCorrect = numCorrect + 1
   End If
   q2Answered = True
   DoingWell
End Sub

Sub DoingWell()
   MsgBox ("You are doing well, " & userName)
End Sub

Sub WrongAnswer1() 'ADDED to replace WrongAnswer
   If q1Answered = False Then
      numIncorrect = numIncorrect + 1
   End If
   q1Answered = True
   DoingPoorly
End Sub

Sub WrongAnswer2() 'Same as WrongAnswer1 with 1 changed to 2
   If q2Answered = False Then
      numIncorrect = numIncorrect + 1
   End If
   q2Answered = True
   DoingPoorly
End Sub

Sub DoingPoorly()
   MsgBox ("Try to do better next time, " & userName)
End Sub

Sub Feedback()
   MsgBox ("You got " & numCorrect & " out of " _
      & numCorrect + numIncorrect & ", " & userName)
End Sub
```

The most significant additions are the new variables q1Answered and q2Answered and the special right and wrong answer procedures for each question. The variables keep track of which questions have already been answered. q1Answered is True if question 1 has been answered, and it is False if question 1 has not been answered. q2Answered is True if question 2 has been answered, and it is False if question 2 has not been answered. If you have more than two questions, you need a q3Answered, q4Answered, etc.; that is, you need one variable for each question. These variables are declared at the beginning with the `Dim` statements:

```
Dim q1Answered As Boolean
Dim q2Answered As Boolean
```

Then, in `Initialize` they are initialized (set to `False` because none of the questions have been answered yet):

```
q1Answered = False
q2Answered = False
```

Remember that if you have more questions, you need to repeat both of these sets of statements for each additional variable.

Next, we need our specialized `RightAnswer` and `WrongAnswer` procedures. `RightAnswer1` is tied to the right answer button for question 1. `WrongAnswer1` is tied to the wrong answer button(s) for question 1. `RightAnswer2` and `WrongAnswer2` are for question 2. And, if we had more questions, `RightAnswer3` and `WrongAnswer3` would be for question 3; `RightAnswer4` and `WrongAnswer4` would be for question 4; etc.

These procedures simply check the appropriate variable to see if the question has been answered. If it hasn't (`If q1Answered = False Then`), we update the score (`numCorrect = numCorrect + 1` or `numIncorrect = numIncorrect + 1`). Regardless of whether or not it has been answered before, we set the variable to `True` (e.g., `q1Answered = True` for question 1) and give the appropriate feedback (calling `DoingWell` or `DoingPoorly`).

Short-Answer Quiz Questions

The above examples can be extended very easily to include short-answer questions. If we were to add a third question that was short answer, we would first need the variable `q3Answered`, just like `q1Answered` and `q2Answered`, declared with a `Dim` statement and initialized in the `Initialize` procedure. We would also need the procedures `RightAnswer3` and `WrongAnswer3`, just like `RightAnswer1` and `WrongAnswer1` (except using `q3Answered` instead of `q1Answered`). Then we would need a procedure to ask a question and judge the answer:

```
Sub Question3()
   Dim answer

   answer = InputBox(Prompt:="What is the capital of Maryland?", _
      Title:="Question 3")
   If answer = "Annapolis" Then
      RightAnswer3
   Else
      WrongAnswer3
   End If
End Sub
```

This procedure uses the variable `answer` to store the answer typed by the student. Because only this procedure needs to know about it, it can be declared inside the procedure (`Dim answer`). Next, we use `InputBox`, just like in the `YourName` procedure, to ask the student to type the answer, which is stored in the variable `answer`.

In our multiple-choice questions, buttons were tied to our `RightAnswer` and `WrongAnswer` procedures. With a short-answer question, we don't have buttons to call these procedures, so we use an `If` statement. If the answer is right, call the appropriate `RightAnswer` procedure; if the answer is wrong, call the appropriate `WrongAnswer` procedure.

The last thing you need is a way for the question to be asked. Figure 7.3 shows an example slide. Just connect the "Click to answer" button to the `Question3` (or whatever number you use) procedure, and when the user clicks on the button, the `InputBox` will pop up asking for an answer. The figure shows a button with the words "Click to answer," but your button can contain the question itself, the word "Question," a question mark, or whatever else you like (as long as the user knows to press the button to get and/or answer the question).

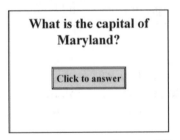

Figure 7.3. Short-Answer Question Slide

Note that this procedure was set up to work with the previous example in which students can answer questions over and over again. To have it work with any other examples, change the calls to `RightAnswer3` and `WrongAnswer3` to `RightAnswer` and `WrongAnswer`.

Do Spelling and Spacing Count?

Now we have a short-answer question, but even people who live in Maryland have trouble spelling "Annapolis." If spelling is important in your test, then leave the `Question3` procedure alone. However, you might be tolerant of several mistakes that your students might make, so you might want to be more lenient. You might want to ignore extra spaces, ignore capitalization, and accept alternative spellings.

Spaces before and after the answer can be handled easily with the `Trim` command. Insert the following line after the `InputBox` statement:

```
answer = Trim(answer)
```

This will take the answer that was typed, remove any spaces at the beginning or end, and put the result (without the extra spaces) back into the answer variable. Trim will turn " Annapolis " into "Annapolis." This will not eliminate any spaces in the middle, so "Ann apolis" will remain "Ann apolis." If for some reason you only want to remove the spaces before the answer or after the answer, use LTrim or RTrim respectively.

If you are not concerned with how your students capitalize their answers, LCase can set the answer to lowercase by adding:

```
answer = LCase(answer)
```

This takes the answer that the student typed, converts all capital letters to lowercase letters, and puts the lowercase version back in the variable answer. This will change "Annapolis," "AnNaPolis," and "AnnApolis" to "annapolis." If you are testing to make sure the student knows to capitalize the first letter of a city name, don't use LCase.

Warning! The answer is now lowercase. This means that your If statement needs to compare it to a lowercase response. If answer = "Annapolis" Then will **never** be True because "annapolis" is not the same as "Annapolis" and LCase changes all capitalizations of "Annapolis" to "annapolis." So even if the student types "Annapolis," LCase will change it to "annapolis" and mark it wrong when comparing it to "Annapolis."

If you are willing to accept alternative spellings or alternative answers, you can test for all the alternatives that you want in your If statement:

```
If answer = "annapolis" Or _
   answer = "anapolis" Or _
   answer = "annappolis" Or _
   answer = "anappolis" Then
```

Include as many or as few different alternatives as you like. Just remember that if you used LCase, all your alternatives must be lowercase.

If we use all our tricks (ignoring extra spaces, accepting any capitalization, and allowing alternative answers), our procedure will look like this:

```
Sub Question3()
   Dim answer

   answer = InputBox(Prompt:="What is the capital of Maryland?", _
      Title:="Question 3")
   answer = Trim(answer)
   answer = LCase(answer)
   If answer = "annapolis" Or _
      answer = "anapolis" Or _
      answer = "annappolis" Or _
      answer = "anappolis" Then
      RightAnswer3
   Else
      WrongAnswer3
   End If
End Sub
```

The exact same procedures can be used for any short-answer question. Simply change the InputBox statement to include your question and change the If statement to include the correct answer(s) for your question.

How Did You Do: Reporting Results to the Teacher

The previous examples concentrated on giving feedback to students by telling them which questions they got right and wrong and what their score is at the end. In this section, you will learn a trick to have your students report results to you. One method of reporting that information is to create a results slide that can be printed. We'll extend the previous examples in two ways to do this:

1. Instead of using a MsgBox to announce the results, we will create a slide that announces the results. The slide will include a button for printing.

2. We will not only keep track of right and wrong answers but specifically what the answer was that was typed. This will allow our results page to print a list of answers that were given.

The most significant changes to the code are related directly to our two extensions:

1. We will add the procedures PrintablePage to create the slide with the results, PrintResults to print the results on the printer, and StartAgain to delete the results slide and go back to the beginning.

2. We will add variables to keep track of which answers were selected first. For this example, we will use the three questions from the previous example so we will have three variables: answer1, answer2, and answer3. These variables will be used to print the students' answers on the printable page.

Here is the complete code (new lines and procedures are indicated by the comment 'ADDED):

```
Dim numCorrect As Integer
Dim numIncorrect As Integer
Dim userName As String
Dim q1Answered As Boolean
Dim q2Answered As Boolean
Dim q3Answered As Boolean
Dim answer1 As String 'ADDED
Dim answer2 As String 'ADDED
Dim answer3 As String 'ADDED
Dim printableSlideNum As Long 'ADDED

Sub GetStarted()
   Initialize
   YourName
   ActivePresentation.SlideShowWindow.View.Next
End Sub

Sub Initialize()
   numCorrect = 0
   numIncorrect = 0
   q1Answered = False
   q2Answered = False
   q3Answered = False
   printableSlideNum = ActivePresentation.Slides.Count + 1 'ADDED
End Sub

Sub YourName()
   userName = InputBox(Prompt:="Type your name")
End Sub

Sub DoingWell()
   MsgBox ("You are doing well, " & userName)
End Sub

Sub DoingPoorly()
   MsgBox ("Try to do better next time, " & userName)
End Sub

Sub Answer1GeorgeWashington()
   If q1Answered = False Then
      numCorrect = numCorrect + 1
      answer1 = "George Washington" 'ADDED
   End If
   q1Answered = True
   DoingWell
   ActivePresentation.SlideShowWindow.View.Next
End Sub

Sub Answer1AbrahamLincoln()
   If q1Answered = False Then
      numIncorrect = numIncorrect + 1
      answer1 = "Abraham Lincoln" 'ADDED
   End If
   q1Answered = True
   DoingPoorly
End Sub
```

```
Sub Answer2Two()
   If q2Answered = False Then
      numCorrect = numCorrect + 1
      answer2 = "2" 'ADDED
   End If
   q2Answered = True
   DoingWell
   ActivePresentation.SlideShowWindow.View.Next
End Sub

Sub Answer2Four()
   If q2Answered = False Then
      numIncorrect = numIncorrect + 1
      answer2 = "4"
   End If
   q2Answered = True
   DoingPoorly
End Sub

Sub Question3()
   Dim answer

   answer = InputBox(Prompt:="What is the capital of Maryland?", _
      Title:="Question 3")
   If q3Answered = False Then 'ADDED
      answer3 = answer 'ADDED
   End If 'ADDED
   answer = Trim(answer)
   answer = LCase(answer)
   If answer = "annapolis" Then
      RightAnswer3
   Else
      WrongAnswer3
   End If
End Sub

Sub RightAnswer3()
   If q3Answered = False Then
      numCorrect = numCorrect + 1
   End If
   q3Answered = True
   DoingWell
   ActivePresentation.SlideShowWindow.View.Next
End Sub

Sub WrongAnswer3()
   If q3Answered = False Then
      numIncorrect = numIncorrect + 1
   End If
   q3Answered = True
   DoingPoorly
End Sub

Sub PrintablePage() 'ADDED
   Dim printableSlide As Slide
   Dim homeButton As Shape
   Dim printButton As Shape
```

```
Set printableSlide = _
    ActivePresentation.Slides.Add(Index:=printableSlideNum, _
    Layout:=ppLayoutText)
printableSlide.Shapes(1).TextFrame.TextRange.Text = _
    "Results for " & userName
printableSlide.Shapes(2).TextFrame.TextRange.Text = _
    "Your Answers" & Chr$(13) & _
    "Question 1: " & answer1 & Chr$(13) & _
    "Question 2: " & answer2 & Chr$(13) & _
    "Question 3: " & answer3 & Chr$(13) & _
    "You got " & numCorrect & " out of " & _
    numCorrect + numIncorrect & "." & Chr$(13) & _
    "Press the Print Results button to print your answers."
Set homeButton = _
    ActivePresentation.Slides(printableSlideNum).Shapes.AddShape _
    (msoShapeActionButtonCustom, 0, 0, 150, 50)
homeButton.TextFrame.TextRange.Text = "Start Again"
homeButton.ActionSettings(ppMouseClick).Action = ppActionRunMacro
homeButton.ActionSettings(ppMouseClick).Run = "StartAgain"
Set printButton = _
    ActivePresentation.Slides(printableSlideNum).Shapes.AddShape _
    (msoShapeActionButtonCustom, 200, 0, 150, 50)
printButton.TextFrame.TextRange.Text = "Print Results"
printButton.ActionSettings(ppMouseClick).Action = ppActionRunMacro
printButton.ActionSettings(ppMouseClick).Run = "PrintResults"
ActivePresentation.SlideShowWindow.View.Next
ActivePresentation.Saved = True
End Sub

Sub PrintResults() 'ADDED
    ActivePresentation.PrintOptions.OutputType = ppPrintOutputSlides
    ActivePresentation.PrintOut From:=printableSlideNum, _
        To:=printableSlideNum
End Sub

Sub StartAgain() 'ADDED
    ActivePresentation.SlideShowWindow.View.GotoSlide (1)
    ActivePresentation.Slides(printableSlideNum).Delete
    ActivePresentation.Saved = True
End Sub
```

The most important thing you need to know about this script is how to add more questions. If you understand the explanation of the script below, that is great, and you will have a better ability to change aspects of the script. But if you don't understand the script, you can still add questions. Almost everything you need to do to add questions is the same as in previous sections:

- You will need another RightAnswer and WrongAnswer procedure for each new question. Note that in the earlier examples, for multiple-choice questions, these procedures would be named RightAnswer4 and WrongAnswer4, RightAnswer5 and WrongAnswer5, etc. In this example our procedures are more specific because the answer1, answer2, and answer3 variables must be set to the chosen answers. That is why you need a procedure for each answer. Just follow the examples of Answer1GeorgeWashington and `Answer1AbrahamLincoln` for right and wrong answers respectively. Note that in this example we have added `ActivePresentation.SlideShowWindow.View.Next` to our `RightAnswer` procedures so the presentation automatically goes to the next slide after a correct answer. Leave this out (just like in the previous example) if you want students to stay on the slide until they choose to go forward.

- You will need another `Question` procedure for every short-answer question (e.g., `Question5` or `Question17`).

- You will need another `qAnswered` and `answer` variable (declared with a `Dim` statement and initialized in the `Initialize` procedure) for each new question (i.e., `q4Answered` and `answer4`, `q5Answered` and `answer5`, etc.).

- You will need to add a line to the `PrintablePage` procedure to include the results for each new question (e.g., `"Question 4: " & answer4 & Chr$(13) & _`).

- You will need to add the slides with the questions you are adding, tying the buttons to the appropriate right and wrong answer procedures or the `Question` procedure for a short-answer question.

As a scripter, you do not need to understand the code to be able to use it. If you can follow the above steps to add your own questions, you are in good shape. If you want to understand the code, read on.

Keeping track of the answers in `answer1`, `answer2`, and `answer3` is fairly simple. Inserting a new page for printing and printing it is more complicated. Because we are going to add a slide, we need to know which slide number to add. This is done with the variable `printablePageNum`. In our `Initialize` procedure, we set this variable to one more than the total number of slides that we have (i.e., if we have six slides, this will be set to 7 because the slide we are going to add will be the seventh slide):

```
printableSlideNum = ActivePresentation.Slides.Count + 1
```

The `PrintablePage` procedure creates the page. Figure 7.4 shows an example of this slide.

The following line creates a slide and stores it in the variable `printableSlide`:

```
Set printableSlide = _
    ActivePresentation.Slides.Add(Index:=printableSlideNum, _
    Layout:=ppLayoutText)
```

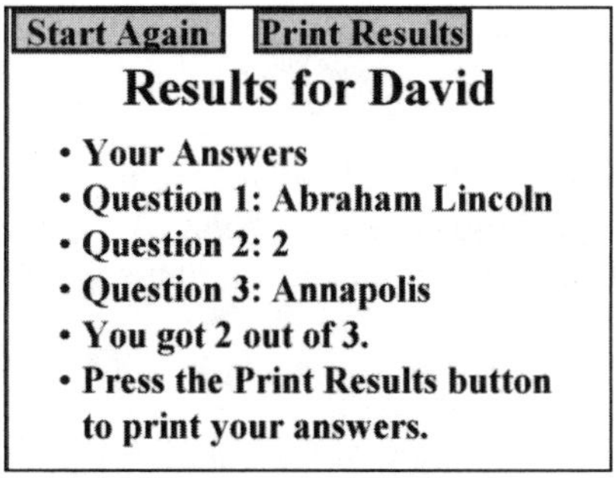

```
| Start Again | Print Results |
```

Results for David

- **Your Answers**
- **Question 1: Abraham Lincoln**
- **Question 2: 2**
- **Question 3: Annapolis**
- **You got 2 out of 3.**
- **Press the Print Results button to print your answers.**

Figure 7.4. Example of Printable Slide

`Index:=printableSlideNum` creates a new slide after the last slide. `Layout:=ppLayoutText` makes the slide a normal Bulleted List slide with two text areas: (1) a title area and (2) a bulleted list area. The following lines set the text in those areas (this is where you would add the answers for more questions):

```
printableSlide.Shapes(1).TextFrame.TextRange.Text = _
    "Results for " & userName
printableSlide.Shapes(2).TextFrame.TextRange.Text = _
    "Your Answers" & Chr$(13) & _
    "Question 1: " & answer1 & Chr$(13) & _
    "Question 2: " & answer2 & Chr$(13) & _
    "Question 3: " & answer3 & Chr$(13) & _
    "You got " & numCorrect & " out of " & _
    numCorrect + numIncorrect & "." & Chr$(13) & _
    "Press the Print Results button to print your answers."
```

`printableSlide.Shapes(1)` refers to the title area of the slide, and `printableSlide.Shapes(2)` refers to the bulleted list area of the slide. Note that if you have several questions, you might want to play with formatting the display of your answers, possibly using a two-column text slide (`ppLayoutTwoColumnText` instead of `ppLayoutText` and putting some text in shape 2 and other text in shape 3) or adjusting the font size of the text area by putting the following line after the above code:

```
printableSlide.Shapes(2).TextFrame.TextRange.Font.Size = 9
```

9 is the size of the font, so you can choose a different number for a smaller or larger font. Note that some versions of PowerPoint (2002 and above) automatically change the font size for you so your text fits the text box. However, if you use those versions, you might consider changing the font yourself in case your presentation is used with an earlier version of PowerPoint.

Next we need to add buttons to our new slide. The following line adds a custom button in the top left of the screen (coordinates 0,0) that is 150 pixels wide and 50 pixels tall. A custom button has no icon in it.

```
Set homeButton = _
    ActivePresentation.Slides(printableSlideNum).Shapes.AddShape _
    (msoShapeActionButtonCustom, 0, 0, 150, 50)
```

Because we stored the button in the variable `homeButton`, we can use that variable to change the attributes of the button. We need to put some text in the button. The text "Start Again" will appear in the button:

```
homeButton.TextFrame.TextRange.Text = "Start Again"
```

Then we make the button clickable and assign a procedure (in this case, the `StartAgain` procedure) to the button:

```
homeButton.ActionSettings(ppMouseClick).Action = ppActionRunMacro
homeButton.ActionSettings(ppMouseClick).Run = "StartAgain"
```

The code for the Print Results button is almost identical, so if you understood the code above you don't need any explanation for the Print Results button.

Finally, we want to go to the slide (`ActivePresentation.SlideShowWindow. View.Next`) that we just created and fool PowerPoint into thinking that the presentation does not need to be saved (`ActivePresentation.Saved = True`— see "Saving and Quitting" in Chapter 8 for more information about this line).

The `PrintResults` procedure has two lines:

```
ActivePresentation.PrintOptions.OutputType = ppPrintOutputSlides
ActivePresentation.PrintOut From:=printableSlideNum, _
    To:=printableSlideNum
```

The first line makes sure that PowerPoint knows it is going to print one slide per page. The second line actually prints the single slide that we just created. If our printable slide is slide number 6 (and thus `printableSlideNum` is 6), that line says to print from slide 6 to 6.

The last procedure is `StartAgain`. This simply goes to the first slide, deletes the slide that was just printed (`ActivePresentation.Slides (printableSlideNum).Delete`), and makes sure that PowerPoint doesn't ask you to save.

You might want to know what buttons will be tied to the last three procedures. `PrintablePage`, instead of the `Feedback` procedure from earlier examples, will be tied to the "How Did I Do" button. But what about the last two procedures? That is a trick question. You don't tie them to any buttons. We have used VBA to create the buttons and tie them to procedures as part of the `PrintablePage` procedure. Creation of the buttons and tying them to procedures is taken care of automatically with our VBA.

Learn First, Ask Questions Later: The Tutorial and Quiz

This chapter has explained several ways to create tests and quizzes. Now we are going to add a tutorial to our presentation. You could do this easily by creating some slides with some information that precede your quiz slides. If each information slide has a button to move forward, students are forced to go through the information slides before reaching the quiz.

This works very well for a simple, linear tutorial. What if your tutorial is more complex? What if your tutorial has several parts, each of which can be reached by a menu? That is not a problem. Simply put buttons on your menu slide for each part of the tutorial and put a button for your quiz on the menu slide as well.

This leaves you with two problems: getting lost in hyperspace and forcing your students to go through the tutorial before taking the quiz. We'll deal with these issues one at a time.

Lost in Hyperspace: Where Have I Been?

In a linear tutorial, that is, one where you force the student to go from one slide to the next to the next, there is no problem with getting lost. Once you allow the student choices about where to go, getting lost is an important concern. That can happen when users don't know where they are, where they are going, where they have been, and how to get where they want to go. In the real world, there are landmarks and street signs to help you get around. Computer screens are often missing those things. Even something as simple as a tutorial with sections linked by a menu can get confusing. The most confusing part of a menu is knowing where you have been: "Did I already do section 2 and section 3 or section 3 and section 4?" One solution to this is to leave some indication in the menu about where the user has been.

There are many ways to do this. One thing that you have probably seen in your Web browser is that it changes the color of visited links: A blue link to another Web page turns purple after you have followed that link. If your menus are all text, PowerPoint will do this automatically for you (although the results might not be exactly what you want). If you use buttons for your menu, one solution is to turn the buttons a different color. For example, you can change the color of the fourth shape on the second slide to magenta with:

```
ActivePresentation.Slides(2).Shapes(4).Fill.ForeColor.RGB = vbMagenta
```

Another possibility is to indicate that a menu item has been visited by putting a symbol next to it, such as a check mark or a smiley face. You might create a tutorial and quiz like the one shown in Figure 7.5 (page 110). This simple tutorial has three parts: The Executive Branch, The Legislative Branch, and The Judicial Branch. Students may choose these parts of the tutorial in any order. Smiling sunshines next to the buttons indicate those sections of the tutorial that have already been completed. The smiling sunshines (or whatever symbols or pictures you like) can be created with any traditional PowerPoint tools (drawing, clip art, inserting a picture, etc.).

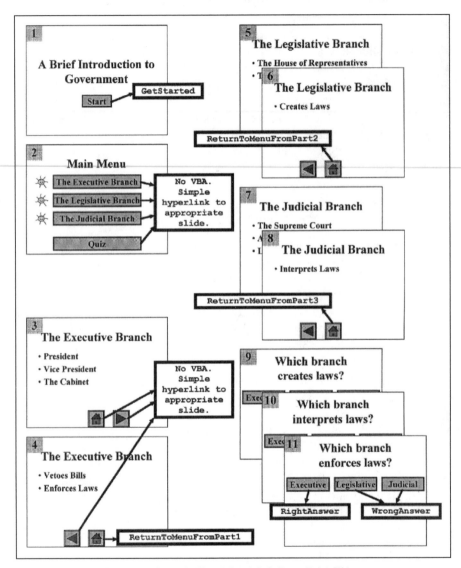

Figure 7.5. Example Tutorial and Quiz PowerPoint Slides

In the figure, slide numbers are shown in the upper left corner of the slide, and the boxes indicate which procedures are tied to which buttons. Notice in the figure that some of the buttons do not use VBA; they use traditional PowerPoint hyperlinks. Figure 7.6 shows the VBA code. Note that the quiz portion of this example is fairly simple (it doesn't keep score), but you can use any of the examples from this chapter and plug the code into the `Initialize` procedure (add that code to earlier `Initialize` procedures; never create two separate `Initialize` procedures) and add the `ReturnToMenuFromPart1`, `ReturnToMenuFromPart2`, `ReturnToMenuFromPart3`, and `JumpToMenu` procedures from Figure 7.6.

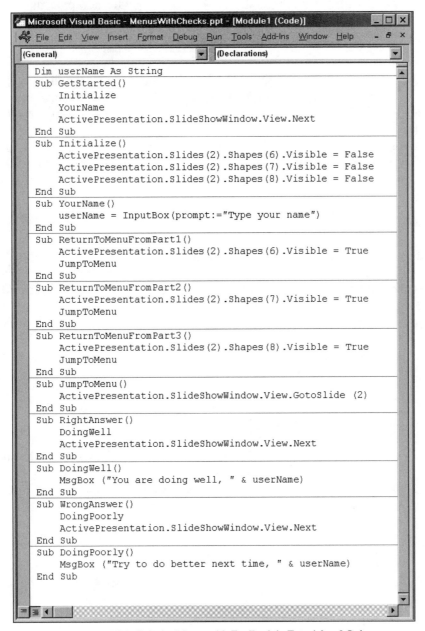

```vba
Dim userName As String
Sub GetStarted()
    Initialize
    YourName
    ActivePresentation.SlideShowWindow.View.Next
End Sub
Sub Initialize()
    ActivePresentation.Slides(2).Shapes(6).Visible = False
    ActivePresentation.Slides(2).Shapes(7).Visible = False
    ActivePresentation.Slides(2).Shapes(8).Visible = False
End Sub
Sub YourName()
    userName = InputBox(prompt:="Type your name")
End Sub
Sub ReturnToMenuFromPart1()
    ActivePresentation.Slides(2).Shapes(6).Visible = True
    JumpToMenu
End Sub
Sub ReturnToMenuFromPart2()
    ActivePresentation.Slides(2).Shapes(7).Visible = True
    JumpToMenu
End Sub
Sub ReturnToMenuFromPart3()
    ActivePresentation.Slides(2).Shapes(8).Visible = True
    JumpToMenu
End Sub
Sub JumpToMenu()
    ActivePresentation.SlideShowWindow.View.GotoSlide (2)
End Sub
Sub RightAnswer()
    DoingWell
    ActivePresentation.SlideShowWindow.View.Next
End Sub
Sub DoingWell()
    MsgBox ("You are doing well, " & userName)
End Sub
Sub WrongAnswer()
    DoingPoorly
    ActivePresentation.SlideShowWindow.View.Next
End Sub
Sub DoingPoorly()
    MsgBox ("Try to do better next time, " & userName)
End Sub
```

Figure 7.6. VBA Code for Menus with Feedback in Tutorial and Quiz

The important parts of this example are shapes 6, 7, and 8 on slide 2 (the menu slide). These are the smiling sunshine pictures that indicate that a section of the tutorial has been completed. Of course, the numbers might change depending on how you create the menu slide, and you might have more menu items and thus more smiling sunshines (or whatever picture you choose).

As the shapes are the important parts, all but one of the new procedures deal with the shapes. The three lines in the Initialize procedure, like

```
ActivePresentation.Slides(2).Shapes(6).Visible = False
```

hide the shapes so that when the student reaches the menu for the first time, the shapes are hidden. If your menu is not on slide 2, change the 2 to something else. In addition, this hides shape 6, so there is one line for each smiling sunshine, each with a different number.

Next we need to show the shapes at the appropriate time. They will be shown when clicking on the button that returns from each part of the tutorial. The three ReturnFromMenuFromPart procedures show the appropriate shape with

```
ActivePresentation.Slides(2).Shapes(6).Visible = True
```

and use JumpToMenu to return to the menu slide.

The tricky part about this example is getting the shape numbers to match the shapes that you use. Figuring out the number of each shape is discussed in "Referencing Objects by Number" in Chapter 6.

If you prefer to change the color of your buttons instead of showing a goofy icon, you can do that with a very small change to the above code. In the Initialize procedure, instead of hiding objects, we can set the color of our menu buttons to blue, for example:

```
ActivePresentation.Slides(2).Shapes(2).Fill.ForeColor.RGB = vbBlue
ActivePresentation.Slides(2).Shapes(3).Fill.ForeColor.RGB = vbBlue
ActivePresentation.Slides(2).Shapes(4).Fill.ForeColor.RGB = vbBlue
```

Note that the shape numbers are 2, 3, and 4 because we are referring to the numbers of the buttons, not the numbers of the smiling sunshines. In our ReturnFromMenuFromPart procedures, we need to change the color of the buttons to a different color, using lines like the following:

```
ActivePresentation.Slides(2).Shapes(2).Fill.ForeColor.RGB = vbMagenta
```

Now that your students know where they have been, in the next section, we will add a few lines so they have to complete the tutorial before taking the quiz.

Hide the Quiz Button

With a button on the menu slide, your students can choose to take the quiz whenever they want. Sometimes this is appropriate; sometimes it is not. For those times when you want your students to complete the tutorial before taking the quiz, we will combine variables (to keep track of what the students have done) with hiding and showing objects (see "Hiding and Showing PowerPoint Objects" in Chapter 6). We will hide the Quiz button on the menu slide until all sections of our tutorial have been visited. Use the code in Figure 7.7 (page 114) to do this. Lines and procedures noted with the comment `ADDED` have been added to the code from the previous example.

Note that this figure does not include the `RightAnswer`, `WrongAnswer`, `DoingWell`, and `DoingPoorly` procedures. Either use the simple ones from the previous example (see Figure 7.6, page 111) or use more complicated quizzes from other examples in this chapter.

If you are adding onto the previous example, all you need to change is the VBA; all the buttons are tied to the same procedures. If you are starting with a new file, use Figure 7.5 (page 110) to guide you in creating the PowerPoint slides and tying the buttons to procedures.

The variables `visitedPart1`, `visitedPart2`, and `visitedPart3` are the keys to this example. They tell us whether the student has completed each part of the tutorial. They are set to `False` in the `Initialize` procedure because no part of the tutorial has been completed. They are set to `True` in the `ReturnToMenuFromPart` procedures to indicate when each part of the tutorial has been completed.

Finally, three new procedures have been added: `HideQuizButton`, `ShowQuizButton`, and `DoWeShowQuizButton`. In my example, the Quiz button is shape number 5 on the menu slide (slide number 2) so I can hide it in `HideQuizButton` with

```
ActivePresentation.Slides(2).Shapes(5).Visible = False
```

Change `False` to `True` to show it, and change 5 to some other number if your Quiz button is not shape 5. Also note that the Quiz button should be hidden at the beginning so `HideQuizButton` is added to `Initialize`.

`DoWeShowQuizButton` asks a three-part question: Is part 1 of the tutorial completed, is part 2 of the tutorial completed, and is part 3 of the tutorial completed? If all three parts have been completed—(`visitedPart1`, `visitedPart2`, and `visitedPart3` have each been set to `True`)—then we show the Quiz button. If any part has not been completed (any `visitedPart` is not `True`), then we hide the Quiz button.

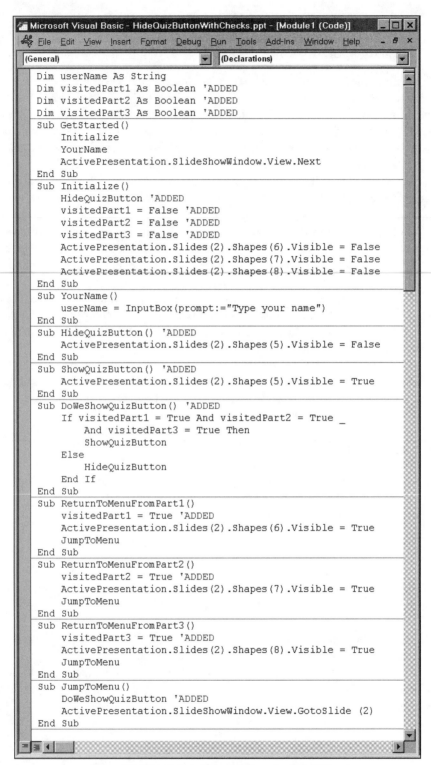

```
Microsoft Visual Basic - HideQuizButtonWithChecks.ppt - [Module1 (Code)]
File  Edit  View  Insert  Format  Debug  Run  Tools  Add-Ins  Window  Help

(General)                              (Declarations)

   Dim userName As String
   Dim visitedPart1 As Boolean  'ADDED
   Dim visitedPart2 As Boolean  'ADDED
   Dim visitedPart3 As Boolean  'ADDED
   Sub GetStarted()
       Initialize
       YourName
       ActivePresentation.SlideShowWindow.View.Next
   End Sub
   Sub Initialize()
       HideQuizButton  'ADDED
       visitedPart1 = False  'ADDED
       visitedPart2 = False  'ADDED
       visitedPart3 = False  'ADDED
       ActivePresentation.Slides(2).Shapes(6).Visible = False
       ActivePresentation.Slides(2).Shapes(7).Visible = False
       ActivePresentation.Slides(2).Shapes(8).Visible = False
   End Sub
   Sub YourName()
       userName = InputBox(prompt:="Type your name")
   End Sub
   Sub HideQuizButton()  'ADDED
       ActivePresentation.Slides(2).Shapes(5).Visible = False
   End Sub
   Sub ShowQuizButton()  'ADDED
       ActivePresentation.Slides(2).Shapes(5).Visible = True
   End Sub
   Sub DoWeShowQuizButton()  'ADDED
       If visitedPart1 = True And visitedPart2 = True _
           And visitedPart3 = True Then
           ShowQuizButton
       Else
           HideQuizButton
       End If
   End Sub
   Sub ReturnToMenuFromPart1()
       visitedPart1 = True  'ADDED
       ActivePresentation.Slides(2).Shapes(6).Visible = True
       JumpToMenu
   End Sub
   Sub ReturnToMenuFromPart2()
       visitedPart2 = True  'ADDED
       ActivePresentation.Slides(2).Shapes(7).Visible = True
       JumpToMenu
   End Sub
   Sub ReturnToMenuFromPart3()
       visitedPart3 = True  'ADDED
       ActivePresentation.Slides(2).Shapes(8).Visible = True
       JumpToMenu
   End Sub
   Sub JumpToMenu()
       DoWeShowQuizButton  'ADDED
       ActivePresentation.SlideShowWindow.View.GotoSlide (2)
   End Sub
```

Figure 7.7. VBA Code to Hide and Show the Quiz Button

If your tutorial has more parts, you will need to do the following:

- Add more variables, such as `visitedPart4` and `visitdPart5`, and declare them with `Dim` statements.

- Initialize the added variables in the `Initialize` procedure, with lines like `visitedPart4 = False`.

- Add more procedures (such as `ReturnToMenuFromPart4` and `ReturnToMenuFromPart5`) to return to the menu from the added parts of the tutorial. Be sure to tie the menu buttons to those parts of the tutorial.

- Add more parts to the `If` question in `DoWeShowQuizButton`. For example:

```
If visitedPart1 = True And visitedPart2 = True _
   And visitedPart3 = True And visitedPart4 = True _
   And visitedPart5 = True Then
```

- Add more smiling sunshine pictures next to the additional menu buttons. Hide them in the `Initialize` procedure and show them in the additional `ReturnToMenuFromPart` procedures.

Of course, this same structure does not need to be used for a tutorial and quiz; it could be used for anything with several parts. If you want your students to complete certain parts before completing some other parts, you can use exactly the same code.

Conclusion

You now have seen several examples of ways to create tutorials and quizzes. You can create different kinds of questions and keep and report scores in different ways. In the next chapter, you learn a few more scripting tricks and get some more explanation about some programming structures.

Exercises to Try

🐾 In the section "Try Again and Again: Answer Again After It's Right," we created a simple multiple-choice quiz that only counts the student's first try on each question. Try to add two more multiple-choice questions to the quiz. Remember that you will need additional variables q3answered and q4answered as well as RightAnswer3, WrongAnswer3, RightAnswer4, and WrongAnswer4 procedures.

🐾 In the section "Short-Answer Quiz Questions," we added short-answer questions to our multiple-choice quiz. Try adding two more short-answer questions to your quiz. Remember that you will need additional Question, RightAnswer, and WrongAnswer procedures.

🐾 In the section "How Did You Do: Reporting Results to the Teacher," we created a slide with the results that was ready to be printed. Follow the directions in that section to add two additional questions to your quiz. One should be a multiple-choice question, and the other should be a short-answer question.

🐾 In the section "Learn First, Ask Questions Later: The Tutorial and Quiz," you created a simple tutorial and quiz with the shapes hidden and shown—to indicate which sections of the tutorial were completed—and a Quiz button that is hidden until all sections of the tutorial are finished. Add a fourth section to your tutorial and use one of the more complex quiz structures (at least something that keeps score) for your quiz.

8

More Tricks for Your Scripting Bag

Introduction

In Chapter 7 you used all the tricks you had learned in previous chapters to create quizzes and tests. This chapter will add to your scripting bag of tricks to help you do more with the examples from previous chapters, create some of your own examples, and understand some of the things you have already used. You will learn more about If statements and loops (like the While loops you have already seen) and about timed functions, automatically saving or not saving your presentation, naming objects and slides, and random numbers. The chapter concludes with a complete example that uses random numbers to randomly show different questions from a large pool.

Vocabulary

- Array
- Conditional
- Dirty
- Infinite loop

- Loop
- Nested If
- Parameter
- Stopping condition

Conditionals: The `If` Statement

It is common to want to do one thing under certain circumstances and something else under other circumstances. If it is raining, we will play inside. Otherwise, we will play outside. We like to do this in VBA as well. We might say:

```
If raining = True Then
    PlayInside
Else
    PlayOutside
End If
```

The `If` statement asks a question. If the answer is yes, we do the first thing. If the answer is no, we do what comes after the `Else`. The above code is exactly the same as the English sentences:

```
If it is raining Then
    We will play inside
Otherwise
    We will play outside
```

The question can be anything that returns a `True` or `False` answer. We might compare the value of a variable to something. For example:

```
If numCorrect > 6 Then
    MsgBox("You got a lot of questions right.")
Else
    MsgBox("You can do better than that.")
End If
```

In this case, if the variable `numCorrect` (presumably that was used by some other procedures to count the number of questions that were answered correctly) is greater than 6, a `MsgBox` will pop up saying "You got a lot of questions right." If the variable `numCorrect` is not greater than 6 (it is 6 or less), then the `MsgBox` will say "You can do better than that."

This can be extended to check more than one thing using `ElseIf`. You might say: if it is raining, we will play inside; if it is snowing, we will build snowmen; otherwise, we will play baseball.

```
If raining = True Then
    PlayInside
ElseIf snowing = True Then
    BuildSnowmen
Else
    PlayBaseball
End If
```

In this case, we ask one question. If the answer is yes, we do the first thing. If the answer is no, we ask a second question. If the answer to the second question is yes, we do the second thing. If the answer to the first question is no, and the answer to the second question is no, we do the third thing. Note, we can ask as many questions as we want by putting more and more ElseIf statements. Imagine a grading program that converts numbers to letter grades:

```
Sub WhatsMyGrade()
    If gradeNum >= 90 Then
        MsgBox("You got an A")
    ElseIf gradeNum >= 80 Then
        MsgBox("You got a B")
    ElseIf gradeNum >= 70 Then
        MsgBox("You got a C")
    ElseIf gradeNum >= 60 Then
        MsgBox("You got a D")
    Else
        MsgBox("You got an F")
    End If
End Sub
```

This assumes that a variable named gradeNum has been given a value somewhere else. It then asks the question, is this grade greater than or equal to 90? If the answer is yes, it pops up a box with the message "You got an A," and it stops. However, if the answer is no, it asks the next question: is this grade greater than or equal to 80? If the answer to this question is yes, it pops up a box with the message "You got a B," and it stops. It keeps asking questions as long as the answers are no. If all the answers are no, it reaches the Else statement and pops up a box with the message, "You got an F."

Note that you can do more than one thing in response to a yes answer. You might, for example, pop up a MsgBox and then move to the next slide under one condition, but pop up a different MsgBox and then move to the previous slide under a different condition:

```
If gradeNum >= 90 Then
    MsgBox ("You got an A.")
    ActivePresentation.SlideShowWindow.View.Next
Else
    MsgBox ("You need to work harder.")
    ActivePresentation.SlideShowWindow.View.Previous
End If
```

Because you can do several things in response to a yes answer, you can do several complicated things. The above example uses two simple statements, but you can have as many statements as you want. Some of these statements might be complicated structures like loops (see the next section) and other If statements. When you put an If block inside an If block, it is called a nested If. If the answer to your question is yes, you might want to ask other questions:

```
If gradeNum >= 90 Then
    MsgBox ("You got an A.")
    If previousGradeNum >= 90 Then
       MsgBox ("Good job. Two A grades in a row!")
    End If
    ActivePresentation.SlideShowWindow.View.Next
Else
    MsgBox ("You need to work harder.")
    ActivePresentation.SlideShowWindow.View.Previous
End If
```

Pay careful attention to the way this example is indented. Although you don't have to type it indented in this way, it is much easier to understand with the indenting. You can see that the question is asked: Is gradeNum greater than 90? Everything between the first If and the Else is indented to show that it is what to do if the answer is yes. Part of what to do is to ask another question. That question asks if previousGradeNum also is greater than 90. This question will only get asked if gradeNum is greater than 90. The indenting helps to see the nesting. It is particularly helpful if the nested If block is more complicated, with its own Else, for example. The Else should always be lined up with the If with which it goes.

The If statement is very powerful. It is one of the things that allows for interaction. Without conditional statements, every user would do exactly the same thing as the previous user.

Looping

If statements allow you to make choices based on whether or not a condition is true. Looping allows you to do something over and over again. How many times is based on a condition, that is, a question like what you ask in an If statement. This is known as the stopping condition. In some types of loops (such as a While loop), this question is phrased as a *keep going* question, and in other types of loops (such as a For Next loop), the condition is based on how many times you say you want to loop. However the question is phrased, the loop needs to know when to stop.

While Loops

There are several types of loops, and you might want to explore different ones, but once you know one, you can do just about anything you might want to do. Let's look at the While loop. The While loop asks a question and keeps looping *while* the answer to the question is yes. My four-year-old daughter might ask "Is it still raining?" She might ask this over and over again until it has stopped raining. As long as it is raining, she will add another block to her tower and ask again:

```
While StillRaining
    AddBlockToTower
Wend
PlayOutside()
```

In this case, the question is: Is it still raining? If the answer is yes, add another block to the tower. The Wend statement stands for *While END* and simply limits the loop. Whatever is between the While and Wend statements will happen over and over again until the answer to the question is no. Many things can happen between a While and Wend; it is not limited to one statement. This loop will keep executing as long as it is still raining. Once it stops, the answer to the question will be no, and whatever is after the Wend will be executed. In this case, my daughter will finally go play outside.

We could use this to ask a question until the right answer is entered. For example:

```
Sub HowManyPlanets()
   Dim answer As String

   answer = ""
   While answer <> "nine" And answer <> "9" And answer <> "Nine"
      answer = InputBox _
         ("How many planets are there in our solar system?")
   Wend
End Sub
```

In this example, the procedure HowManyPlanets contains a While loop with a slightly complicated question. The question basically asks: Is the answer wrong? That is, is whatever the user typed not "nine," "9," or "Nine"? If it is not any of those, it will ask for the answer again and again and again until one of those answers is entered in the InputBox.

Sometimes we might not want our users to get stuck in a loop if they really don't know the answer. We might want to limit the number of times we ask the question. In this example, the user will be asked three times, so our While question checks to be sure that the answer is wrong and that we have asked fewer than three times.

```
Sub HowManyPlanets()
   Dim answer As String
   Dim count As Integer

   answer = ""
   count = 0
   While answer <> "nine" And answer <> "9" And answer <> "Nine" _
      And count < 3
      answer = InputBox _
         ("How many planets are there in our solar system?")
      count = count + 1
   Wend
End Sub
```

The variable count is a number (an Integer). We started it out as 0 (count = 0) because at the beginning, we haven't asked at all. Then we check to see whether the answer is not one of the right answers (nine, 9, or Nine), and we also check whether the count is still less than 3. If the answer is still wrong, and the count is still less than 3, we ask for the answer again and add 1 to count (count = count + 1). Once we have asked three times, count will be 3. Then, the question in our While statement will be no because count < 3 will be False. In that case, we will stop looping.

When the conditions are complicated, we might want to do what we have done with the YourName procedure (see Chapter 5):

```
Sub YourName()
    Dim done As Boolean

    done = False
    While Not done
        userName = InputBox(prompt:="Type your name", _
            Title:="Input Name")
        If userName = "" Then
            done = False
        Else
            done = True
        End If
    Wend
End Sub
```

In this procedure, we use the variable done to determine whether we are finished looping. The If block could have all been included in the While statement, eliminating the need for done. This would have made for short VBA code, but it would have been very difficult to understand, particularly if the stopping condition was more and more complicated. Setting up an If block allows you to check as many conditions as you like and set done based on those conditions. Then, the only question for While is: Are we done or not? If we are not done, keep looping.

Do Loops

Do loops are similar to While loops. They allow you to specify either a While condition (keep going *while* something is True) or an Until condition (keep going *until* something is True). They also let you specify the condition (ask the stopping question) at the beginning or the end. If the condition is at the beginning, the loop might never run (not even once). If the condition is at the end, the loop will always run at least once. Here are some simple examples:

```
Do
    answer = InputBox("How many planets are in the solar system?")
Loop Until answer = "9"

Do
    answer = InputBox("How many planets are in the solar system?")
Loop While answer <> "9"

Do While count < 3
    answer = InputBox("What do you like to eat?")
    count = count + 1
Loop
```

```
Do Until count >= 3
    answer = InputBox("What do you like to eat?")
    count = count + 1
Loop
```

In the first example, the loop will run at least once and ask the question: How many planets are in the solar system? After running the loop once, it will check to see if answer is 9. If it is, it will stop. If it isn't, it will loop *until* the answer is 9.

In the second example, the loop will run at least once and ask the question: How many planets are in the solar system? After running the loop once, it will check to see whether answer is not 9. It will keep looping *while* the answer is not 9. Note, this works exactly the same as the first example, but sometimes it is easier to ask a positive question than a negative question, particularly if the question has many parts with And and Or.

In the third and fourth examples the condition will be checked before the loop runs. In the third example, the loop will only run if count is less than 3, and it will keep looping *while* count is less than 3. In the fourth example, the loop will stop running if count is greater than or equal to 3, and it will keep looping *until* count is greater than or equal to 3. Like the first two examples, these examples have exactly the same results, but sometimes it is easier to ask a positive question, and sometimes it is easier to ask a negative question.

For Next Loops

Sometimes you have a specific number of times you want to loop. For Next loops allow you to do this and keep a count of the loop. This could be done with a While or Do loop by adding one to a count variable inside the loop, but it can be easier with a For Next loop.

A simple example of a For Next loop follows:

```
For i = 1 To 10
    MsgBox("Counting..." & i)
Next i
```

This uses the variable i and counts from 1 to 10. That is, i starts out at 1, and the loop keeps looping (everything between the For line and the Next line is run) over and over again, adding 1 to i, up to and including the time that i becomes 10. Next i says to go back to the beginning of the loop and increase i. As with all the other loops, you can put as many lines as you like between the For line and the Next line, and all those lines will be executed over and over again.

For Next, Do, and While loops can get more complicated, but these basic loops should suit most of your purposes.

Infinite Loops

Before we leave looping, a word of warning about infinite loops: In all of our loops, we have set stopping conditions; that is, we have told the loop when to stop looping. What if the stopping condition is never met? Then you have an infinite loop, a loop that never stops. Here is a simple example (don't type this):

```
While 8 > 7
   MsgBox ("Eight is still greater than seven.")
Wend
```

Because 8 > 7 is always True (i.e., 8 is always greater than 7), this loop will never stop. Usually, you won't have something so obvious. You will either type something wrong (perhaps > when you meant <), or you will have a complicated expression with variables, and you won't realize that the condition for stopping never can be met.

If you get stuck in an infinite loop, it will appear that PowerPoint has frozen. In all likelihood, you will have to force PowerPoint to quit. On a Windows computer, you can use Ctrl-Alt-Delete (i.e., hold down the Ctrl and Alt keys while hitting the Delete key). Depending on the version of Windows you are running, you will either restart your computer or be given the option to stop an unresponsive application (PowerPoint, in this case). If you are on a Macintosh, you will have to hit Command-Option-Esc (i.e., hold down the Command and Option keys while hitting the Esc key; note that the Command key is the one with the picture of the apple on it). If you do this, you will lose any changes you made to your presentation since you saved it last. That is why it is very important to save changes often, particularly when you are working with loops. In fact, when testing out a loop, you should probably save your changes before you put PowerPoint in Slide Show View.

Parameters

Sometimes a procedure has all the information it needs when you write it. Sometimes it gets information from variables where we have stored information (as long as the variables are declared at the beginning of the module). At other times we want to give a procedure extra information as we go. We can do this with something called a parameter. A parameter is extra information sent to a procedure when it is called. We have used parameters when calling procedures (something as simple as a MsgBox takes a parameter: the text to display), but we have not used parameters in procedures we have written. Parameters are a very useful tool for programmers, but they can be a bit tricky. Following is a brief explanation of parameters, so when you see them in examples (such as the timed functions in the next section), you'll understand them.

Imagine that you wanted to put up a MsgBox with different messages for different occasions. Perhaps the message is the same except for one thing. For example, you might want to say, "You are doing well, Ella" at some point and "You are doing poorly, Ella" at another time. We have done this with two separate procedures in the past, but we could write one procedure with a parameter:

```
Sub Doing(doingHow As String)
    MsgBox ("You are doing " & doingHow & ", " & username)
End Sub
```

For something this simple, the parameter may not be worth the effort, but it can be very useful if the procedure that takes the parameter is more complicated. In this case doingHow is the parameter. It is a String because it is declared in the Sub statement to be a String, so another procedure would call doingHow with a String in parentheses. For example Doing("well") would pop up a MsgBox that says, "You are doing well, Ella" (assuming the userName was "Ella") . This might be called from a procedure that included the following If block:

```
If numCorrect > 10 Then
    Doing ("superbly")
ElseIf numCorrect > 8 Then
    Doing ("well")
ElseIf numCorrect > 5 Then
    Doing ("OK")
ElseIf numCorrect > 3 Then
    Doing ("Poorly")
Else
    Doing ("Very Poorly")
End If
```

Parameters can be of any type. We used a String in this example, but you can pass various kinds of numbers or Booleans or even objects such as shapes. You can pass more than one parameter as well if you need different kinds of information passed to a procedure, but for most of your purposes, if you need a parameter at all, one will suffice. Parameters can be tricky and complicated, so we will not use them a lot, but now you have a basic understanding of how they work in case you see them in some examples.

Timed Functions

Most actions in PowerPoint happen because the user did something, such as pressing a button to go to another slide. Sometimes, however, you want things to happen whether or not the user has done anything. For example, you might want a sound to start playing a few seconds after the slide is shown. You might want the presentation to go from slide to slide on its own. You might want information to pop up on the screen, then go away, and then have other information pop up on the screen.

As soon as the user clicks on a button tied to a script with timing features (such as the button to go to another slide), you can start anything happening after any length of time. Of course, the standard "Custom Animation" choice from the Slide Show menu can allow objects to appear with timing, but you might want to do more. If you want something to happen after a short delay, you can use the following procedure:

```
Sub Wait()
    waitTime = 5
    start = Timer
    While Timer < start + waitTime
        DoEvents
    Wend
End Sub
```

This procedure waits five seconds. `Timer` is a function that returns the number of seconds since midnight (e.g., at 12:01 A.M., `Timer` will return 60). `waitTime` is a variable used to tell how many seconds to wait (change the number 5 to any number to have this procedure wait that number of seconds). At the beginning of the procedure, the variable `start` is set to the current time in seconds (as returned by `Timer`). Next, we loop until the current time is less than the time we started plus the `waitTime` (which is five seconds in our example). Inside the loop (between the `While` statement and the `Wend` statement), we run `DoEvents`. This lets VBA check to see if anything else is happening, particularly things that the user might do, such as hit the Escape key or click on another button. If you don't want the user to do anything while you are waiting, leave out `DoEvents`.

Be careful! If you make a mistake (perhaps you set the `waitTime` to five million seconds instead of five seconds or you mistyped `Timer` in the `Do While` statement), you could end up in an infinite loop, essentially freezing PowerPoint. If you feel you must stop the user from doing anything while VBA waits, leave `DoEvents` in your procedure until you are sure everything works. Once you are certain everything works, delete the `DoEvents` line. This will allow you to stop your presentation by hitting the Escape key while you are still testing your procedure.

Before we continue, get a new PowerPoint presentation and type the `Wait` procedure. Then add the following procedure:

```
Sub HelloWaitGoodbye()
    MsgBox ("Hello")
    Wait
    MsgBox ("Goodbye")
End Sub
```

When you run `HelloWaitGoodbye`, you should see a `MsgBox` that says "Hello." After you click OK to dismiss the `MsgBox`, you should see a `MsgBox` that says "Goodbye," but only after a delay of five seconds.

Now suppose that you want to wait, but not always for five seconds. You could write several different procedures (`Wait5`, `Wait10`, `Wait60`, etc.) to wait different amounts of time, but we can use a simple parameter to write one procedure that can wait different amounts of time.

```
Sub Wait(waitTime As Long)
   start = Timer
   While Timer < start + waitTime
      DoEvents
   Wend
End Sub
```

In this procedure, instead of setting the `waitTime` to five, we call `Wait` with however long we want to wait (e.g., `Wait (60)` would wait sixty seconds).

Timed functions are useful if you want to give your users a chance to do something before moving on. For example, you might display a text box, wait a short time, then display a second text box. This allows the user to focus on the first text box before getting too much information. Be careful with timed functions, because different people read at different speeds. If you set your wait times too long, some people will get restless waiting for the next thing to happen. If you set them too short, some people will not have time to finish the first thing.

Some timing can be done automatically without VBA. You can use Custom Animation to have things appear and disappear as much as you like. However, as with many things that you can do without VBA, you might find that you can do more with VBA. For example, you might ask the user how fast to go:

```
speed = InputBox ("How fast do you read [fast, medium, slow]?")
```

Now when it is time to wait, you might do something like the following:

```
If speed = "fast" Then
   Wait (5)
ElseIf speed = "medium" Then
   Wait (10)
Else
   Wait (15)
End If
```

You should note that wait times are approximate. This does not work well if you need precise timing, but it should do roughly what you want.

Saving and Quitting

When you use VBA to change your presentation in any way (including adding shapes, hiding shapes, changing text, etc.), PowerPoint recognizes that your project has been changed. Whenever a project has been changed, PowerPoint wants to save it. If you don't save it, and you exit PowerPoint, PowerPoint will ask you if you want to save. This is a good thing if you are designing a project and forgot to save before exiting. This might not be such a good thing if one of your students is running your project.

As the designer of an interactive multimedia project, you should know when you want to save and when you don't. In "How Did You Do: Reporting Results to the Teacher" in Chapter 7, we added a slide to report the results, but we didn't want to save the slide. In this case, PowerPoint knows that the presentation has been changed, so we needed to make it think that it was not changed. Of course, changes that PowerPoint thinks need to be saved do not have to be as large as adding a slide. Changes as small as hiding or showing an object, such as a shape that indicates the student has visited part of the tutorial in "Learn First, Ask Questions Later" in Chapter 7, will make PowerPoint think your presentation needs to be saved.

In other cases, we might want the changes to be saved. In Chapter 10 is an example in which important slides are being added to the presentation. As users go through the project, they might be asked for information, which is stored on a newly created slide. Later, the designer will go through the presentation and look at those slides . . . only if they were saved.

Fortunately, it is very easy to control whether or not your presentation is saved. Four simple procedures will help you:

```
Sub MakeNotDirty()
   ActivePresentation = True
End Sub

Sub Save()
   ActivePresentation.Save
End Sub

Sub Quit()
   Application.Quit
End Sub

Sub QuitAndSave()
   Save
   Quit
End Sub
```

In computer terms, a presentation that is changed but not saved is called *dirty*. The status of the current presentation (whether it is dirty or not, i.e., whether it has been changed or not since the last time it was saved) is stored in the variable `ActivePresentation.Saved`. Even if the presentation has been changed, we can fool PowerPoint into thinking that it hasn't been changed by setting the `ActivePresentation.Saved` to `True` as in the `MakeNotDirty` procedure above. If you call this procedure (or simply put the line `ActivePresentation.Saved = True` into some other procedure), PowerPoint will not ask you if you want to save the presentation when you quit. Be sure you do this every time you make a change because the next change you make will make the presentation dirty again, setting `ActivePresentation.Saved` back to `False`.

You probably want to do this right away when you make a change. In fact, you should do it in the procedure that makes the change. For example:

```
Sub StartAgain()
    ActivePresentation.SlideShowWindow.View.GotoSlide (1)
    ActivePresentation.Slides(printableSlideNum).Delete
    ActivePresentation.Saved = True
End Sub
```

This procedure is from the example in "How Did You Do: Reporting Results to the Teacher" in Chapter 7. This procedure jumps to the first slide and deletes the last slide (which had been created temporarily in an earlier procedure). Once it deletes the last slide, the presentation is dirty, but we don't want anyone to be asked to save it. By setting `ActivePresentation.Saved` to `True`, the students won't be asked.

For the cases where you want to save a presentation, you can use the `Save` procedure above. As long as the place where the presentation is running is a location that can be saved (unlocked disk, network folder where the user has write privileges, etc.), `Save` will save the presentation without the user even knowing (unless it is saving something to a slow device like a floppy disk, in which case it might take a few seconds to save). You would use this (or simply the line `ActivePresentation.Save`) immediately after doing something that you want saved. An example of this can be found in Chapter 10:

```
Sub WorkTogether()
    GetNameEmailIdea
    GoToWorkTogether
    AddWorkTogetherSlide
    Save
End Sub
```

In this example, information is collected (using the `GetNameEmailIdea` procedure), the presentation jumps to another slide (using the `GoToWorkTogether` procedure), and a new slide is added to the presentation (using the `AddWorkTogetherSlide` procedure, which is where the presentation becomes dirty). Finally, the presentation is saved (using the `Save` procedure). The saving happens automatically without the user's knowledge. Of course, the `Save` procedure from above must be included in your VBA module.

Finally, you might want to quit the presentation (possibly when a user presses an Exit button). If you weren't worried about saving, you could simply hyperlink a button to End Show (using traditional PowerPoint and no VBA). If you are worried about saving, you will need something like the last two procedures. `Quit` will quit the presentation without saving and without asking the user whether or not to save. Be careful with this. If you are trying out your `Quit` procedure while you are creating your presentation and you haven't saved, your changes will be lost. This includes changes to your VBA code. Therefore, you should always save your presentation before trying it out.

`QuitAndSave` simply calls our `Save` procedure before quitting, so the presentation will be saved. Note that `Save` ignores whether or not the presentation is dirty; it saves regardless. Thus, you don't want to save if you have made changes that you don't want saved (even if you have called `MakeNotDirty`).

Being sure that changes are saved or not saved as you, the designer, know they should be is very important. Your students won't know whether they should save or not, and they shouldn't be bothered by being asked. The procedures in this section will help you manage the saving or not saving of your presentation.

What's in a Name? Finding and Changing Object and Slide Names

Object Names

In Chapter 6 we discussed how to reference objects by their names, and we noted how difficult it is to remember the name of an object. The following scripts can be used to find the name of an object and set the name of an object. Note that all other scripts in this book are designed to be run in Slide Show View. These scripts are designed to be run in Edit View.

The two procedures that we need are `GetObjectName` and `SetObjectName`. `GetObjectName` finds out what the name of an object is. `SetObjectName` asks you to type a new name for an object.

If you run the `GetObjectName` script while an object is selected, a `MsgBox` will pop up with the object's name. If you run `SetObjectName`, an `InputBox` will allow you to enter a name for an object. These scripts check to make sure that one and only one object is selected, because you can't get or change the name of more than one object at a time.

```
Sub GetObjectName()
   If ActiveWindow.Selection.Type = ppSelectionShapes _
      Or ActiveWindow.Selection.Type = ppSelectionText Then
      If ActiveWindow.Selection.ShapeRange.count = 1 Then
         MsgBox (ActiveWindow.Selection.ShapeRange.Name)
      Else
         MsgBox ("You have selected more than one shape.")
      End If
   Else
      MsgBox ("No shapes are selected.")
   End If
End Sub

Sub SetObjectName()
   Dim objectName As String

   If ActiveWindow.Selection.Type = ppSelectionShapes _
      Or ActiveWindow.Selection.Type = ppSelectionText Then
      If ActiveWindow.Selection.ShapeRange.count = 1 Then
         objectName = InputBox(prompt:="Type a name for the object")
         objectName = Trim(objectName)
```

```
         If objectName = "" Then
             MsgBox ("You did not type anything. " & _
                "The name will remain " & _
                ActiveWindow.Selection.ShapeRange.Name)
         Else
             ActiveWindow.Selection.ShapeRange.Name = objectName
         End If
      Else
         MsgBox _
             ("You can not name more than one shape at a time. " _
             & "Select only one shape and try again.")
      End If
   Else
      MsgBox ("No shapes are selected.")
   End If
End Sub
```

If you are trying to understand these procedures, pay careful attention to the nested `If` statements and how they are indented in the example.

The heart of these procedures is `ActiveWindow.Selection.` `ShapeRange.Name`. This looks at the `Name` property of the currently selected shape. In `GetObjectName`, we simply return this name in a `MsgBox`. In `SetObjectName`, we set this with whatever is typed in an `InputBox`. The rest of each of the procedures is to make sure an object is selected and to clean up what you typed for the object's name.

If you run the `GetObjectName` script while an object is selected, a `MsgBox` will pop up with the object's name. You can then use this name in quotes instead of an object's number. For example, if you wanted to hide an object named "Picture 6," you can use:

```
ActivePresentation.SlideShowWindow.View.Slide. _
   Shapes("Picture 6").Visible = False
```

As you recall from Chapter 6, once you add an object to your slide, its name, unlike its number, will not change unless you change it, so this line of code will always work even if you change the animation order or delete other objects on the slide. Even if you don't name your own objects, each new object that is added to a slide is given a name that is different from all other objects that have ever been added to that slide.

When you run `SetObjectName`, an `InputBox` will allow you to enter a name for an object. `Trim` is used to delete any extra spaces before and after the name you type. The procedure also checks to make sure you typed something, because you don't want to give an object a blank name.

`GetObjectName` and `SetObjectName` check to make sure that one and only one object is selected, because you can't get or set the name of more than one object at a time. If you are looking for a simpler way to do the same things, you can try the following scripts, but you are responsible for making sure that you have selected one and only one object.

```
Sub GetObjectName()
   MsgBox (ActiveWindow.Selection.ShapeRange.Name)
End Sub

Sub SetObjectName()
   Dim objectName As String

   objectName = InputBox(prompt:="Type a name for the object")
   objectName = Trim(objectName)
   If objectName = "" Then
      MsgBox ("You did not type anything. The name will remain " & _
         ActiveWindow.Selection.ShapeRange.Name)
   Else
      ActiveWindow.Selection.ShapeRange.Name = objectName
   End If
End Sub
```

If you try to run either of these procedures without having one object selected, you will get an error message. If you try to give an object the same name as another object on that slide, you will also get an error message, so be sure to give each object on a slide a different name.

Because these procedures run in Edit View in PowerPoint (not from Slide Show View or from the VBA Editor), we cannot create a button on a slide to run them. The easiest way to run a script in Edit View is to select "Macro" from the Tools menu and choose "Macros" from the flyout menu (or hit Alt-F8 on a Windows computer or Option-F8 on a Macintosh). Select the procedure name that you want to run, and click on the Run button (see Figure 8.1).

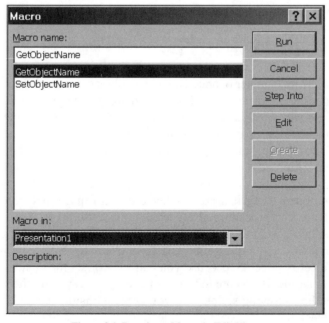

Figure 8.1. Running a Macro in Edit View

Slide Names

Just as object numbers can change, slide numbers can change as well. If you are trying to go to a particular slide and you use a slide number, you might have a problem if you delete or insert slides before that slide. Slide names never change unless you change them. When a slide is created, it is assigned a name (Slide1, Slide2, Slide3, etc.). These names are assigned in the order the slide is inserted, not the order in which the slide is within the presentation. For example, if you create a slide, it will be named "Slide1." If you create another slide, it will be named "Slide2." If you create a third slide between "Slide1" and "Slide2," it will be the second slide in the presentation, but it will be named "Slide3."

If you move slides around a lot, you will have a hard time remembering their names. Use `GetSlideName` and `SetSlideName` to find out the name of a slide and change the name of a slide:

```
Sub GetSlideName()
   MsgBox ActiveWindow.View.Slide.Name
End Sub

Sub SetSlideName()
   Dim slideName As String

   slideName = InputBox(prompt:="Type a name for the slide")
   slideName = Trim(slideName)
   If slideName = "" Then
      MsgBox ("You did not type anything. " & _
      "The name will remain " & _
      ActiveWindow.View.Slide.Name)
   Else
      ActiveWindow.View.Slide.Name = slideName
   End If
End Sub
```

These procedures are very similar to `GetObjectName` and `SetObjectName`. They also run in Edit View of PowerPoint, so they must be run with the "Macros" option from the "Macro" flyout menu of the Tools menu (see Figure 8.1).

Once you have a slide's name, you can use it in two ways. If you want to access the slide, such as to hide and show objects on it, you can use the name in place of the slide number. For example, in "Learn First, Ask Questions Later" in Chapter 7, we wanted to hide the marks on the menu slide to indicate that those sections of the tutorial had not been visited. We used:

```
ActivePresentation.Slides(2).Shapes(6).Visible = False
```

This hides shape 6 on slide 2. If we were to name our menu slide "Menu" and the object to be hidden "MenuMark1," we could use the following line instead:

```
ActivePresentation.Slides("Menu").Shapes("MenuMark1").Visible = False
```

It is slightly more difficult to jump to a named slide. `ActivePresentation.` `SlideShowWindow.View.GotoSlide` requires a number; that is, it cannot use the name of the slide in place of the number. Fortunately, we can get the slide number by using the name. To jump to the slide named "Menu," we could use the following two lines:

```
theSlideIndex = ActivePresentation.Slides("Menu").SlideIndex
ActivePresentation.SlideShowWindow.View.GotoSlide (theSlideIndex)
```

Although this is a little more complicated than simply using a number, it is a lot safer because slide names never change unless you change them.

You never have to use object names or slide names. You can do everything you want with numbers. However, as you make more complicated presentations with more slides and more objects, and you begin to change slides and objects around, using names will save you a lot of grief. When you move objects, delete slides, reorder slides, insert slides, change the animation order of objects, etc., your slide names will remain the same, and your VBA code will continue to work.

Arrays

Computer programs can use many different kinds of data structures. Understanding data structures is an important part of computer programming. However, throughout this book I have avoided turning you into a programmer and only shown you what you need to know to be a scripter. The topic of data structures is something you can avoid, but if you understand some basic data structures, they can make your life easier. In fact, some of the examples that you have seen could have been simpler with some more advanced data structures. I have made some earlier examples longer so that they would be easier to understand.

Data structures are a way to store information. In Chapter 5 we used the box analogy to show how variables can be used to store information, but sometimes information can be stored more easily in something other than a single box. A collection of numbered boxes might be more suitable. This collection of numbered boxes is an array. You might think of an array as an egg carton, with sections for each of several eggs.

In several earlier examples, such as the example in "Try Again and Again: Answer Again After It's Right" from Chapter 7, we created our own numbered variables. In that example, we used `q1Answered` and `q2Answered` to store the information about whether question 1 was answered and whether question 2 was answered. If we had more questions, we would add more variables. This is easy to understand but difficult to type, particularly if we have a lot of questions. This could be simplified with an array.

The first step is to declare the array. Suppose we have five questions. Without an array we would do the following to declare our five variables:

```
Dim q1Answered As Boolean
Dim q2Answered As Boolean
Dim q3Answered As Boolean
Dim q4Answered As Boolean
Dim q5Answered As Boolean
```

If we were to use an array, we would have one line:

```
Dim qAnswered(5) As Boolean
```

This will give us an array that contains six boxes, numbered 0 through 5: qAnswered(0), qAnswered(1), qAnswered(2), qAnswered(3), qAnswered(4), and qAnswered(5). Note that we really only need five boxes in our example, and we got six. There are many ways to avoid getting the extra box, but unless you are an aspiring programmer, the easiest thing to do is simply ignore box number 0.

Now, we can shorten our Initialize procedure. It won't be shorter with two questions (or significantly shorter with five), but when you create something with ten or twenty questions it will be much shorter:

```
Sub Initialize()
   Dim i As Long

   numCorrect = 0
   numIncorrect = 0
   For i = 1 to 5
      qAnswered(i) = False
   Next i
End Sub
```

This procedure uses a For loop, just like what we saw above in "Looping." It loops through each of the members of the qAnswered array and sets each to False. In the original version, every time you added a new question, you would need to add a new Dim statement and a new line in Initialize. Now, the only thing you have to change is the number "5" in your Dim statement and in the For line of your Initialize procedure.

Having a separate variable for each question was only a little inconvenient. The biggest inconvenience was having a separate RightAnswer and WrongAnswer procedure for each question. We needed this

1. to assign True or False to the correct qAnswered variable;

2. to know which question was being answered so we could know which was the appropriate qAnswered variable for number 1; and

3. in later examples, to assign the actual answer to the correct answer variable.

Our array takes care of number 1. Number 2 can be handled easily if our questions are all in order. In our examples with the questions beginning on slide 2, each question is one less than the slide number (i.e., question 1 is on slide 2, question 2 is on slide 3, etc.), so to get the question number, we simply subtract one from the slide number (`ActivePresentation.SlideShowWindow.View.Slide.SlideIndex - 1`). We'll take care of number 3 in the next section.

Using the `Dim` statements and `Initialize` procedure from above and the `GetStarted`, `YourName`, `DoingWell`, and `DoingPoorly` procedures from any of the earlier examples, we can use the following `RightAnswer` procedure and `WrongAnswer` procedure to replace all the specialized `RightAnswer` and `WrongAnswer` procedures. The only thing you ever have to change is the number 5 in the `Dim` statement and the `Initialize` procedure. Just make this number equal to the number of questions you have.

```
Sub RightAnswer()
   Dim thisQuestionNum As Long

   thisQuestionNum = _
      ActivePresentation.SlideShowWindow.View.Slide.SlideIndex - 1
   If qAnswered(thisQuestionNum) = False Then
      numCorrect = numCorrect + 1
   End If
   qAnswered(thisQuestionNum) = True
   DoingWell
End Sub

Sub WrongAnswer()
   Dim thisQuestionNum As Long

   thisQuestionNum = _
      ActivePresentation.SlideShowWindow.View.Slide.SlideIndex - 1
   If qAnswered(thisQuestionNum) = False Then
      numIncorrect = numIncorrect + 1
   End If
   qAnswered(thisQuestionNum) = True
   DoingPoorly
End Sub
```

I Don't Know How Many Questions:
ReDim to the Rescue

It is very nice to cut down on the amount of VBA code that needs to be changed, but wouldn't it be nice to have the above procedures work without changing any VBA code? The problem is that we need to know how many questions we have so we can declare and initialize our qAnswered array. VBA is very nice about this; if you don't know how many items you need in an array, it lets you tell it whenever you know. We can declare the array with the following `Dim` statement (note that nothing is between the parentheses):

```
Dim qAnswered() As Boolean
```

This says that we need an array `qAnswered` to hold `Boolean` values, but we don't know how many values we'll need to hold. When we do know how many values, we can use the `ReDim` statement to tell VBA.

The question is, how and when do we know how many values we need? The answer is that we know right away, and we can tell by how many slides we have. In our example, we have five question slides, one title slide, and one results slide, for a total of seven slides. That is, all but two of our slides (the title slide and the results slide) are question slides. Thus our total number of questions is the total number of slides minus two:

```
ActivePresentation.Slides.Count - 2
```

We can use this in our `Initialize` procedure by assigning this value to a variable (we'll use `numQuestions`), using `ReDim` to tell VBA how many items we need in `qAnswered`, and using this value in our `For` loop to initialize each item.

```
Sub Initialize()
    Dim i As Long
    Dim numQuestions As Long

    numCorrect = 0
    numIncorrect = 0
    numQuestions = ActivePresentation.Slides.Count - 2
    ReDim qAnswered(numQuestions)
    For i = 1 To numQuestions
        qAnswered(i) = False
    Next i
End Sub
```

Two words of warning about `ReDim`:

1. Because you have already told VBA what kind of variable `numQuestions` is with the `Dim` statement, you do not tell it again (notice that `ReDim` leaves off the `As Boolean` in our example).

2. `ReDim` erases the contents of the array, so be sure that you use it before you put anything in the array.

Using the new `Dim` statement and the new `Initialize` procedure, you never have to change the VBA. This makes it easier for you because you can add and change questions with no VBA changes, and it turns this into a powerful tool for your students; they can make their own quizzes that use your VBA (see Chapter 10 for more about templates). Some of you will want to teach your students VBA, but most of you will not. If you can write the code, all they have to do is create the questions and tie the buttons to the `RightAnswer` and `WrongAnswer` procedures.

Short-answer questions will still need VBA to check the answer. You can either:

- stick to multiple-choice questions and never touch the above code, or

- use short-answer questions by writing `Question1`, `Question2`, `Question3`, etc., procedures for each short-answer question but having each `Question` procedure call `RightAnswer` and `WrongAnswer`, not specialized `RightAnswer1` and `WrongAnswer1`, `RightAnswer2` and `WrongAnswer2`, `RightAnswer3` and `WrongAnswer3`, etc., procedures.

With either choice, your VBA is greatly simplified. You could probably even teach your students to copy and paste new question procedures, simply changing the number of the question in the `Sub` line and the text for the question and right answer.

Which Button Did I Press?

The above example works very well when you don't need to keep track of which answer was chosen. But what about the example from Chapter 7 in "How Did You Do: Reporting Results to the Teacher"? In that example, each answer needs to be stored. Short-answer questions don't have much of an issue because you already have to use VBA to check the answer, so you can easily stick the answer in a variable at that time. But multiple-choice questions are more of a problem. In the example in Chapter 7, we had a different procedure for each button. This is easy to understand, but the amount of code can be overwhelming if you have a lot of questions.

Fortunately, there is a VBA trick that can save us. Try assigning the following procedure to a button. In fact, create a slide with several buttons, add different text to each button, and attach this procedure to each button:

```
Sub WhichButton(answerButton As Shape)
   Dim theAnswer As String
   theAnswer = answerButton.TextFrame.TextRange.Text
   MsgBox ("You chose " & theAnswer)
End Sub
```

This uses a special trick with parameters (see "Parameters") . When a button is pressed, it can pass the button itself as a parameter to the procedure that called it. Normally, we use VBA to pass parameters (by putting them in parentheses when we call a procedure), but in this case, clicking the button passes the parameter. We just have to set up our procedure to store the parameter. In this example, we used the variable `answerButton`. Once we have a pointer to the button itself (i.e., `answerButton`), we can get the text that is in the button with `answerButton.TextFrame.TextRange.Text`. If you have put the answer in the text of the button, you can use that to get the answer that was chosen.

Now we can store the answers for a printable slide without adding any extra code for each multiple-choice question and without adding very much extra code for each short-answer question. Our code for the simple three-question example is a bit longer, but as you add more questions, the overall code will be much shorter. In fact, just like the previous example, if you only use multiple-choice questions, you do not have to change the code at all when you add questions.

The new code follows. The `GetStarted`, `YourName`, `DoingWell`, and `DoingPoorly` procedures are the same ones we have used many times before. We can also use the new `RightAnswer` and `WrongAnswer` procedures from the previous example. However, these procedures will not be tied directly to buttons. Instead, for multiple-choice questions we will add two new procedures, `RightAnswerButton` and `WrongAnswerButton`, that will be tied to the buttons with right and wrong answers. Here are the new procedures, together with the `Dim` statements and a slightly modified `Initialize` procedure. Use `GetStarted`, `YourName`, `DoingWell`, and `DoingPoorly` procedures from any earlier example, and use `RightAnswer` and `WrongAnswer` procedures from the previous example (see page 136), along with the following:

```
Dim numCorrect As Integer
Dim numIncorrect As Integer
Dim userName As String
Dim qAnswered() As Boolean
Dim answer() As String 'Array to store answers
Dim numQuestions As Long
Dim printableSlideNum As Long

Sub Initialize()
   Dim i As Long

   numCorrect = 0
   numIncorrect = 0
   printableSlideNum = ActivePresentation.Slides.Count + 1
   numQuestions = ActivePresentation.Slides.Count - 2
   ReDim qAnswered(numQuestions)
   ReDim answer(numQuestions)
   For i = 1 To numQuestions
      qAnswered(i) = False
   Next i
End Sub

Sub RightAnswerButton(answerButton As Shape)
   Dim thisQuestionNum As Long

   thisQuestionNum = _
      ActivePresentation.SlideShowWindow.View.Slide.SlideIndex - 1
   answer(thisQuestionNum) = answerButton.TextFrame.TextRange.Text
   RightAnswer
End Sub
```

```
Sub WrongAnswerButton(answerButton As Shape)
   Dim thisQuestionNum As Long

   thisQuestionNum = _
      ActivePresentation.SlideShowWindow.View.Slide.SlideIndex - 1
   answer(thisQuestionNum) = answerButton.TextFrame.TextRange.Text
   WrongAnswer
End Sub
```

You have already seen (in the `RightAnswer` and `WrongAnswer` procedures) `thisQuestionNum` used to store the number of the current question. The only new code is the `Dim` statement to declare `answer` as an array and the `answerButton.TextFrame.TextRange.Text` to get the text from the button that was pressed (as described above). In addition, we have done a bit of restructuring. In the original example in Chapter 7, each button had its own procedure, and that procedure took care of storing the answer, keeping track of which question was answered, and keeping score. We have divided up that work. Now the `RightAnswerButton` and `WrongAnswerButton` procedures take care of storing the answer, and the `RightAnswer` and `WrongAnswer` procedures take care of keeping track of which question was answered and keeping score.

This division of labor will be important when we add a short-answer question. For short-answer questions, we are going to need a `Question` procedure for each question. That procedure will ask the question, judge the answer, and store the answer. When it figures out if the answer was right or wrong, it will call the `RightAnswer` or `WrongAnswer` procedure. So we need the following procedures:

- Each short-answer question needs its own `Question` procedure (`Question1`, `Question2`, `Question3`).

- All the multiple-choice questions need one `RightAnswerButton` and one `WrongAnswerButton` procedure, which will be tied to every button with a right and wrong answer, respectively.

- All the questions need one `RightAnswer` and `WrongAnswer` procedure, which is called from `RightAnswerButton`, `WrongAnswerButton`, and each `Question` procedure.

Next, our `Question` procedures need a slight modification so they can store the answer in the `answer` array. Here is an example procedure for `Question3`:

```
Sub Question3()
   Dim theAnswer As String
   Dim thisQuestionNum As Long

   thisQuestionNum = _
      ActivePresentation.SlideShowWindow.View.Slide.SlideIndex - 1
```

```
    theAnswer = InputBox(Prompt:="What is the capital of Maryland?", _
       Title:="Question " & thisQuestionNum)
    If qAnswered(thisQuestionNum) = False Then
       answer(thisQuestionNum) = theAnswer
    End If
    theAnswer = Trim(theAnswer)
    theAnswer = LCase(theAnswer)
    If theAnswer = "annapolis" Then
       RightAnswer
    Else
       WrongAnswer
    End If
End Sub
```

The changes to this procedure from the example in Chapter 7 are simply to account for the fact that answer is an array now. Nothing else has changed.

The final change to our code comes in the PrintablePage procedure. You could simply change this procedure to use the array (using answer(1), answer(2), answer(3), instead of answer1, answer2, answer3), but this would require you to change the procedure every time you add a new question. The purpose of complicating our code with arrays was to eliminate any unnecessary changing of code. Our new PrintablePage procedure follows:

```
Sub PrintablePage()
    Dim printableSlide As Slide
    Dim homeButton As Shape
    Dim printButton As Shape

    Set printableSlide = _
       ActivePresentation.Slides.Add(Index:=printableSlideNum, _
       Layout:=ppLayoutText)
    printableSlide.Shapes(1).TextFrame.TextRange.Text = _
       "Results for " & userName
    printableSlide.Shapes(2).TextFrame.TextRange.Text = _
       "Your Answers" & Chr$(13)
    For i = 1 To numQuestions
       printableSlide.Shapes(2).TextFrame.TextRange.Text = _
          printableSlide.Shapes(2).TextFrame.TextRange.Text & _
          "Question " & i & ": " & answer(i) & Chr$(13)
    Next i
    printableSlide.Shapes(2).TextFrame.TextRange.Text = _
       printableSlide.Shapes(2).TextFrame.TextRange.Text & _
       "You got " & numCorrect & " out of " & _
       numCorrect + numIncorrect & "." & Chr$(13) & _
       "Press the Print Results button to print your answers."
    printableSlide.Shapes(2).TextFrame.TextRange.Font.Size = 9
    Set homeButton = _
       ActivePresentation.Slides(printableSlideNum).Shapes _
       .AddShape(msoShapeActionButtonCustom, 0, 0, 150, 50)
    homeButton.TextFrame.TextRange.Text = "Start Again"
    homeButton.ActionSettings(ppMouseClick).Action = ppActionRunMacro
    homeButton.ActionSettings(ppMouseClick).Run = "StartAgain"
    Set printButton = _
       ActivePresentation.Slides(printableSlideNum).Shapes _
       .AddShape(msoShapeActionButtonCustom, 200, 0, 150, 50)
    printButton.TextFrame.TextRange.Text = "Print Results"
    printButton.ActionSettings(ppMouseClick).Action = ppActionRunMacro
```

```
    printButton.ActionSettings(ppMouseClick).Run = "PrintResults"
    ActivePresentation.SlideShowWindow.View.Next
    ActivePresentation.Saved = True
End Sub
```

Other than using the answer array, the main change to this procedure is that we must loop through all the answers so we can display them. We cannot put a line for each answer, as we have done in the past, because we do not know how many questions we will have. Instead, we use a For loop to cycle through the answers and add them to the slide:

```
For i = 1 To numQuestions
    printableSlide.Shapes(2).TextFrame.TextRange.Text = _
        printableSlide.Shapes(2).TextFrame.TextRange.Text & _
        "Question " & i & ": " & answer(i) & Chr$(13)
Next i
```

In English, this code says: For each answer in the answer array, take all the text we have already put in Shape2 of the slide (printableSlide. Shapes(2).TextFrame.TextRange.Text) and add (&) to that the question number ("Question " & i) and the answer with a new line (answer(i) & Chr$(13)). After the For loop, we also add to all of that the score and the instructions for printing the slide.

Finally, if you are using a version of PowerPoint that does not automatically change the size of the text to fit the text box, you will want to be sure to change the size of the text so you can fit more than three or four answers on the slide:

```
printableSlide.Shapes(2).TextFrame.TextRange.Font.Size = 9
```

Just change the 9 to a smaller number if you have more questions.

As a scripter, your burning question should be: How do I add questions to my presentation? If you have put all the above code in your presentation, you must do the following things to add questions:

1. For each multiple-choice question, do not touch the VBA; just add the question slide and tie the button for the right answer to RightAnswerButton and the buttons for wrong answers to WrongAnswerButton.

2. For each short-answer question, add a slide with the question and tie the question button to a new procedure that is exactly like Question3, except that it will have a different number for the name of the procedure (Question4, Question5, etc.) and it will change the text of the question in the InputBox statement and the correct answer(s) to check for in the If statement.

3. If you have a lot of questions, change the font size of the text box in the PrintablePage procedure to 9 or smaller.

Random Numbers

Random numbers are a powerful tool. Often you know exactly what you want in your presentation and in exactly what order. At other times you want to mix things up randomly. For example, you might want to practice addition facts, but you don't want to specify every possible combination of one-digit numbers. Instead you want the computer to randomly generate problems for you. In another example, you might have a large pool of questions, but you only want to ask a few that are randomly selected. This section explores these examples.

To have the computer generate random numbers, you need to know three things: `Randomize`, `Rnd`, and `Int`. For you math purists, computers cannot generate truly random numbers, but they can come close enough for almost any purpose.

To be sure they are close enough for our purposes, we need to make sure that they are not the same every time. That is why we start with a `Randomize` statement. Just put this somewhere where it will be run before you need any random numbers (such as in your `Initialize` procedure). Imagine that the computer has a big deck of cards with numbers on them. When you ask for a random number, it picks the first card off the top of the deck and gives you the number on it. When you ask for another random number, it picks the next card. This deck of cards starts out in the same order every time, so every time you start the presentation and ask for a bunch of cards, you will get the same cards. This isn't very good. What we need is to shuffle the cards. `Randomize` shuffles the cards. We only need to do this once when we run the presentation, because the deck of cards is very large. That is why we do this in our `Initialize` procedure.

Next, we want to get a random number. This is done with the `Rnd` statement. You could have a procedure that includes:

```
myRandomNumber = Rnd
MsgBox(myRandomNumber)
```

This will pop up a `MsgBox` with a random number in it. The problem is that the number that is generated is somewhere between 0 and 1. Normally, we want random numbers that are positive integers (you know: 1, 2, 3, 4, 5, 6, . . .). Have no fear. That is where `Int` comes in. `Int` takes a real number and chops off everything after the decimal point. For example, `Int(3.1415926)` returns 3, and `Int(.4567)` returns 0. We can generate a random number between 0 and 9 with:

```
myRandomDigit = Int(10 * Rnd)
```

By multiplying a number between 0 and 1 by 10, we get a number from 0 up to 9.99999999. By taking the `Int` of that we get 0, 1, 2, 3, 4, 5, 6, 7, 8, or 9. We can get a random number in any range by using the following formula:

```
Int((upper - lower + 1) * Rnd + lower)
```

upper is the biggest number you would want, and lower is the smallest number you would want. For our 0 through 9 example, we would have Int((9 - 0 + 1) * Rnd + 0) or Int(10 * Rnd) + 0) or just Int(10 * Rnd). If we wanted numbers from 1 to 100, we would have Int((100 - 1 + 1) * Rnd + 1) or Int(100 * Rnd + 1). If we wanted numbers from 50 to 100, we would have Int((100 - 50 + 1) * Rnd + 50) or Int(51 * Rnd + 50). Don't worry if you don't quite understand the math; just use the simple formula, and you will be fine.

Randomly Generated Questions

Let's use random numbers with a simple example. In this example, we will want to randomly generate one-digit addition problems. We will have a title card with a button linked to GetStarted and a question card with a button linked to RandomQuestion. The code follows:

```
Sub GetStarted()
   Initialize
   ActivePresentation.SlideShowWindow.View.Next
End Sub

Sub Initialize()
   Randomize
End Sub

Sub RandomQuestion()
   Dim first As Integer
   Dim second As Integer
   first = Int(10 * Rnd)
   second = Int(10 * Rnd)
   answer = InputBox("What is " & first & " + " & second & "?")
   If answer = first + second Then
      DoingWell
   Else
      DoingPoorly
   End If
End Sub

Sub DoingWell()
   MsgBox ("Good job")
End Sub

Sub DoingPoorly()
   MsgBox ("Try to do better")
End Sub
```

GetStarted is the same as our usual GetStarted although in this example we don't use the student's name so we don't call YourName. You could add the Dim userName, the YourName procedure, and appropriate references to userName in `DoingWell` and `DoingPoorly` if you want. Because we are not keeping track of anything, `Initialize` just shuffles the deck by calling `Randomize`.

The heart of the procedure is `RandomQuestion`. This generates two random numbers from 0 to 9 and stores them in the variables `first` and `second`. If you want them to be something other than from 0 to 9, use the earlier formula to figure it out. Next, it puts up an `InputBox` asking for the student to type the sum of those two numbers. Then, it checks to see whether the answer was right by comparing what was typed to `first + second`, which is the right answer. You can change this to multiplication or subtraction by using * or – instead of +. You can add a `third` variable to make this into a problem with three numbers. You can even display the problem in a text box by using some of the tools for manipulating text from Chapter 6. You might have an easier time formatting the numbers into columns if you use a text box or more than one text box.

Keeping Score

With some minor modifications, we can plug `RandomQuestion` into some of our other quizzes from Chapter 7. We'll start by keeping score. Start with the code from "Keeping Score" in Chapter 7 (see Figure 7.1, page 93). Add the following `RandomQuestion` procedure (this is the same as the previous `RandomQuestion` procedure, except that it calls `RightAnswer` and `WrongAnswer` instead of `DoingWell` and `DoingPoorly`):

```
Sub RandomQuestion()
   Dim first As Integer
   Dim second As Integer
   first = Int(10 * Rnd)
   second = Int(10 * Rnd)
   answer = InputBox("What is " & first & " + " & second & "?")
   If answer = first + second Then
      RightAnswer
   Else
      WrongAnswer
   End If
End Sub
```

Add `Randomize` to the `Initialize` procedure. Remove `ActivePresentation.SlideShowWindow.View.Next` from `RightAnswer` and `WrongAnswer` so it does not automatically advance to the next slide.

For this to work properly, you need three slides: a title slide, a question slide, and a feedback slide. The title slide has a button tied to `GetStarted`. The question slide has a button tied to `RandomQuestion` and a button that goes to the next card. And the feedback slide has a button tied to `Feedback`.

If you are adventurous, you might try to eliminate the feedback slide and keep a running total in a text box on the slide. After each question, update the text in the text box. You already have the number of correct and incorrect answers stored in `numCorrect` and `numIncorrect`. You simply need to use this to update a text box after each question is answered.

Try Again: Answer Until It's Right

Next, we can try to force the student to answer until the question is right, only counting the first try. This time, start with the code from "Try Again: Answer Until It's Right" in Chapter 7. Make the exact same changes as above, except use this RandomQuestion procedure:

```
Sub RandomQuestion()
    Dim first As Integer
    Dim second As Integer
    Dim done As Boolean

    done = False
    first = Int(10 * Rnd)
    second = Int(10 * Rnd)
    While Not done
        answer = InputBox("What is " & first & " + " & second & "?")
        If answer = first + second Then
            RightAnswer
            done = True
        Else
            WrongAnswer
        End If
    Wend
End Sub
```

This uses a While loop similar to what is used for short-answer questions. The random numbers are generated before the While loop so that the same question is asked over and over again until it is answered correctly.

If you want to try to create a printable page with the results, you can try that on your own. Start with the version of that from this chapter in "Arrays." Keep in mind that simply listing the answers might not be helpful because the questions are randomly generated. You might want to add another array to keep track of the questions so you can add the questions and answers to your slide.

Choose Questions Randomly from a Pool

My daughter is learning to read. Although I am generally opposed to computer use by five-year-olds, my daughter is fascinated with the computer, and I thought I could use it with her to help her read. I took the words she was working with in school and the reading sentences her teachers sent home and created a presentation. The presentation contains a few sentences and a multiple-choice question on each slide. Throughout the year, I added to the slides, but I did not want her to go through each slide every time. I wanted to limit her time on the computer, so I wanted the computer to randomly select five questions for her to answer. The presentation uses an array to keep track of which questions have been answered (so no question is repeated in each set of five) and random numbers to pick which question to present next. The code for this presentation can be found in Figure 8.2.

```
Microsoft Visual Basic - EllaCanReadSimple.ppt - [Module1 (Code)]            _ □ ×
 File   Edit   View   Insert   Format   Debug   Run   Tools   Add-Ins   Window   Help    Type a question for help ▼ _ ε ×
(General)                                ▼   RandomNext                              ▼
Dim username As String
Dim visited() As Boolean
Dim numSlides As Long
Dim numRead As Integer
Dim numWanted As Integer
Sub GetStarted()
    Initialize
    YourName
    RandomNext
End Sub
Sub Initialize()
    Randomize
    numWanted = 5
    numRead = 0
    numSlides = ActivePresentation.Slides.Count
    ReDim visited(numSlides)
    For i = 2 To numSlides - 1
        visited(i) = False
    Next i
End Sub
Sub YourName()
    username = InputBox("What is your name?")
End Sub
Sub RightAnswer()
    DoingWell
    visited(ActivePresentation.SlideShowWindow.View.Slide.SlideIndex) = True
    numRead = numRead + 1
    RandomNext
End Sub
Sub WrongAnswer()
    DoingPoorly
End Sub
Sub DoingWell()
    MsgBox ("Good job, " & username & ".")
End Sub
Sub DoingPoorly()
    MsgBox ("Try again, " & username & ".")
End Sub
Sub RandomNext()
    Dim nextSlide As Long

    If numRead >= numWanted Or numRead >= numSlides - 2 Then
        ActivePresentation.SlideShowWindow.View.Last
    Else
        nextSlide = Int((numSlides - 2) * Rnd + 2)
        While visited(nextSlide) = True
            nextSlide = Int((numSlides - 2) * Rnd + 2)
        Wend
        ActivePresentation.SlideShowWindow.View.GotoSlide (nextSlide)
    End If
End Sub
```

Figure 8.2. VBA Code for Selecting Five Questions from a Pool of Questions

This presentation consists of a title slide, a last slide, and as many question slides as we want. The title slide has a button that is tied to the GetStarted procedure. The question slides have buttons for right and wrong answers that are tied to the RightAnswer and WrongAnswer procedures, respectively. The last slide has a button that is hyperlinked to the first slide (no VBA) and plays the applause sound. This version does not keep score.

The key elements of this presentation are the array `visited` and the procedure `RandomNext`. `visited` has an element for each question. Actually, it has an element for each slide, but the first and last elements are ignored. The elements are each set to `False` in `Initialize`. When a question is answered correctly, the element of `visited` for that question is set to `True` in the `RightAnswer` procedure. In addition, one is added to `numRead`, a variable that keeps track of how many questions have been read.

`RandomNext` is used to go to the next question instead of `ActivePresentation.SlideShowWindow.View.Next`. In the past, the next question has always been the next slide. Now, we want to randomly select a slide, so we can't simply go to the next slide. `RandomNext` first checks to see whether we have answered five or more questions. Just in case the presentation doesn't have five questions, it also checks to be sure we haven't answered as many questions as there are:

```
If numRead >= numWanted Or numRead >= numSlides - 2 Then
```

`numWanted` was set in `Initialize` to be 5; that is, we want to ask five questions at a time. You can change that number in `Initialize` if you want to ask more or fewer than five questions at a time, or you can ask the user how many questions to do (see below).

If we have asked enough questions, `RandomNext` jumps to the last slide. Otherwise, it randomly picks a new slide to jump to. Randomly picking another slide is very easy using `Rnd`, but we want to make sure we are jumping to a slide that we haven't seen yet. First we randomly pick a slide:

```
nextSlide = Int((numSlides - 2) * Rnd + 2)
```

This assigns the randomly chosen slide to `nextSlide`. The `While` loop keeps looping as long as we have seen the chosen slide (`visited(nextSlide) = True`). That is, if we pick slide 7 as our next slide, `visited(7)` will be `True` if we have seen slide 7, so we will keep looping, and pick another slide with `nextSlide = Int((numSlides - 2) * Rnd + 2)`. Once we have picked the next slide, we can go there with:

```
ActivePresentation.SlideShowWindow.View.GotoSlide (nextSlide)
```

That is all you need to choose a few questions from a pool of questions. To add more questions, you don't have to change any VBA at all; just add more question slides between the first and last slide. If you want to ask a different number of questions, you can either change `numWanted = 5` to another number in the `Initialize` procedure, or you can try out the code in the next section.

This is a good place to remind you that you can and should use all the traditional PowerPoint tools at your disposal. For many of the questions I have made for my daughter, I include pictures from clip art for the answers instead of regular buttons. I also use sounds liberally. The most important use of sound (aside from the applause at the end) is sound for difficult words or sentences. If I include a word or sentence that might be beyond my daughter's skills, I add a recorded sound of me reading the word or sentence. She knows that she can click on any speaker icon to have something read to her. While I am not a big fan of bells and whistles, you should use as many traditional features of PowerPoint as you think are appropriate.

Ask How Many Questions You Want

In the above example, a simple line of VBA was used to determine the number of questions to be asked at a time. Perhaps you want the user to pick. To do this, simply replace numWanted = 5 with HowMany in the Initialize procedure, and add the following HowMany procedure:

```
Sub HowMany()
   done = False
   While Not done
      numWanted = InputBox("How many questions would you like?")
      If numWanted >= 1 And numWanted <= 10 Then
         done = True
      Else
         MsgBox ("Pick a number from 1 to 10")
         done = False
      End If
   Wend
End Sub
```

The heart of this procedure is the InputBox statement. That is really all that is needed. However, my daughter might be inclined to type a very large number and get a lot of questions (so she can put off going to bed). The While simply checks to make sure the number chosen is between 1 and 10 inclusive. If you don't care what number is chosen, leave out the While loop. If you want to allow a different range of numbers, change the numbers in the While statement.

Keeping Score

For my daughter at the age of five, I don't keep score, but you might want to report a score at the end. Adding scorekeeping is not hard. We will need numCorrect and numIncorrect to be declared (Dim numCorrect and Dim numIncorrect) at the beginning of the module and initialized in the Initialize procedure (numCorrect = 0 and numIncorrect = 0), just like in any example that keeps score. Because we are asked to repeat a question until it is correct, we need qAnswered to be declared Dim qAnswered at the beginning of the module and initialized in the Initialize procedure (qAnswered = False). Finally, RightAnswer and WrongAnswer need to adjust the score if the question has been answered:

```
Sub RightAnswer()
   If qAnswered = False Then
      numCorrect = numCorrect + 1
   End If
   qAnswered = False
   DoingWell
   visited(ActivePresentation.SlideShowWindow.View.Slide.SlideIndex) _
      = True
   numRead = numRead + 1
   RandomNext
End Sub

Sub WrongAnswer()
   If qAnswered = False Then
      numIncorrect = numIncorrect + 1
   End If
   qAnswered = True
   DoingPoorly
End Sub
```

These are all the same changes that we made when we wanted to keep score in Chapter 7. You should be able to add short-answer questions by using the same Question procedures for each question that you used in Chapter 7.

You now have a powerful tool for randomly selecting slides. Note that these examples used quizzes, but if you understand this code, you can do something very similar to create a random story that picks random slides to go to next. The heart of this is RandomNext as well as the line:

```
visited(ActivePresentation.SlideShowWindow.View.Slide.SlideIndex) = True
```

Together, these will pick a random slide to go to next and mark that you have gone to that slide.

Conclusion

In this chapter you have developed a better understanding of a few VBA tricks we had already used, such as looping and If statements, and you learned several new tricks, including timed functions, arrays, and random numbers. These tricks are beginning to get more complicated than the earlier chapters, so if you don't understand how they work, you can simply type in the VBA code from the examples. If you do understand how they work, you can think of new things that you can do with these tricks—or at least modify the examples to suit your own purposes.

Now that you might be writing some of your own code, or at least typing in long examples, you have a lot of opportunity to make mistakes. Mistakes are common in scripting and programming, and they are called bugs. Fixing mistakes is called debugging. In the next chapter, you will learn some tricks to help you debug your code, that is, fix your mistakes.

Exercises to Try

✥ Create a template of a multiple-choice quiz using the code from this chapter. Teach three of your friends, colleagues, or students to create their own multiple-choice quizzes using your template. Remember that they don't have to change any of the VBA to do this.

✥ Create a template of a quiz with short-answer questions using the code from this chapter. Teach three of your friends, colleagues, or students to create their own quizzes with short-answer questions using your template. Remember that they will have to edit the VBA, so you will have to teach them how to get to the VBA Editor, but they will only have to copy and paste your `Question` code and change the question number, the text of the question, and the answer to the question in VBA.

9

Debugging Tips

Introduction

In Chapter 8 you added to your bag of tricks. Whether you are ready to venture out on your own, writing scripts that are more than minor modifications of the examples in this book, or are simply copying more and more complex examples, you are bound to make mistakes. This chapter describes several ways to track down your mistakes and avoid making mistakes in the first place, and points you to some common mistakes for which you can look when your code seems like it should work, but it doesn't.

Vocabulary

- Bug
- Capitalization
- Compile error
- Commenting out
- Debug
- Indenting
- Run time error

My Scripts Always Work the First Time

If you have tried more than one or two examples in this book, you are almost certain to have made at least one mistake. In computer terms, mistakes are called bugs. This term comes from the time when computers were as big as entire rooms and real bugs were a problem:

American engineers have been calling small flaws in machines "bugs" for over a century. Thomas Edison talked about bugs in electrical circuits in the 1870s. When the first computers were built during the early 1940s, people working on them found bugs in both the hardware of the machines and in the programs that ran them.

In 1947, engineers working on the Mark II computer at Harvard University found a moth stuck in one of the components. They taped the insect in their logbook and labeled it "first actual case of bug being found." The words "bug" and "debug" soon became a standard part of the language of computer programmers. (Smithsonian National Museum of American History, n.d.)

The process of fixing bugs is called debugging. If you follow the examples in this book exactly, debugging is not difficult; you simply compare what you typed to the example and find the difference. Once you get a little more adventurous and try to make a few small changes to the scripts, you will need some ideas to help you solve problems.

Testing for Bugs

There are two main types of bugs: (1) those that cause your script not to work, and (2) those that cause your script to work but not work properly. The first type is easy to detect because you will either get an error message or nothing will happen (see below). The second type is much harder to detect because everything will appear to work fine, but the results you get will not be right (e.g., the computer tells you how many questions were answered correctly, but the number it gives is not the right number). Both kinds of bugs require you to test your project to make sure it is working properly.

When you write a procedure, you should try to tie it to a button as soon as possible. Then go to Slide Show View and click on the button. If you get an error message or, more likely, nothing happens, you know you have a problem. This is probably the first type of error, and you can go back to your script to find out what is wrong.

If something happens, but it is the wrong thing, you know you have a problem. This is the second type of error. Unfortunately, the second type of error is usually harder to spot and requires much more extensive testing as well as paying close attention to what happens. For something as simple as the `DoingWell` procedure, it might be easy to see that you have a problem, but this procedure relies on the `YourName` procedure to give it the correct answer. If `DoingWell` brings up a `MsgBox` with "You are doing well," and no name, there is a problem, but where is it? Before you even track down where the problem is, you must notice that a problem exists. If you are not paying close attention, you will see a `MsgBox` pop up, but you will not notice that anything is wrong.

As our procedures become more and more complicated and more and more interdependent, spotting a problem can be very difficult. If a procedure isn't tied to a button but called from another procedure, you can't simply tie the procedure to a button and expect it to work. A procedure that depends on other things happening first is hard to test. If you tie `DoingWell` to a button and click on the button, you might not get the results you expect, but it might be because something is wrong, or it might be because you haven't clicked on a button that is tied to `YourName` yet. This could be because some of your procedures are written incorrectly, you are testing out an isolated procedure before putting the whole presentation together, or you didn't force the student to type a name before moving through the presentation.

This is an example of why thoroughly testing your procedures is very important. If you create a presentation, you know what you are supposed to do. If you always do what you are supposed to do and everything works, you know the project works when your students always do what they are supposed to do. Do your students always do what they are supposed to do? Of course not. They will get answers wrong. They will click on one button when you gave them directions to click on another button first. They will use arrow keys and the space bar to move to the next slide if you forgot to put your presentation in Kiosk mode. They will click the same button fifty times in a row, just to hear the sound that the wrong-answer buttons make. In short, they will not do everything right, and when you are testing your program, you should not either.

No News Is Bad News

VBA is not very talkative when it comes to bugs. Once it encounters a bug in a procedure, it just stops. You could have a procedure that is 100 lines long, but if there is bug on the first line, the last 99 won't execute. And VBA will be silent. If you're like me, you click on the button again (and again and again and again), muttering to yourself that this has to work. On the one hand, it would be nice if VBA told you something was wrong, a polite `MsgBox` saying, "I'm sorry, but you have a problem in your procedure. I cannot continue." On the other hand, computer error messages are notorious for being incomprehensible. So, would you rather get nothing or "36549 invalid register access"?

Just treat nothing as your private error message. If you expect something and nothing happens, you know something is wrong, and it is time to start looking for bugs.

The Error in Red

Sometimes the VBA Editor will catch an error and highlight it in red. As you type your code and hit the Enter key (Return key on a Macintosh) after you type a line, certain types of errors will turn red. You can also get those same errors to turn red by clicking on any other line in your module. Keep in mind that lines that end with an underscore are continued on the next line, so you have to hit Enter after the whole line is finished, or you have to click on a different line to get the error to turn red.

One common mistake is to type a line and immediately switch back to PowerPoint to test out your procedure. If you do this without hitting Enter or clicking on another line, you will miss the red, and your procedure will not work. The line still will be red when you get back to the VBA Editor, but you will have wasted the time going back to PowerPoint, running your procedure, and scratching your head for a few seconds while trying to figure out what went wrong.

Usually, with errors that turn red, you will also get a message right away that tells you something about the error. For example, Figure 9.1 shows a typical error.

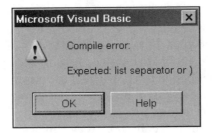

Figure 9.1. Typical Compile Error

This is a compile error. A compile error happens when the computer can't even figure out what to try to do. In this case, it is probably looking for a close parenthesis. It even suggests that that might be the case. A line like the following will generate the error in Figure 9.1:

```
MsgBox ("hello"
```

Sometimes these messages are helpful, and sometimes they are not. Although the message in Figure 9.1 indicates that we are missing a comma or a close parenthesis, sometimes a message like that is the result of some completely different problem.

Try typing the following procedure to add a 16-point star to your current slide:

```
Sub AddStar()
    ActivePresentation.SlideShowWindow.View.Slide.Shapes.AddShape _
        (msoShape16pointStar
End Sub
```

If you hit Enter (or click anywhere else in your module) after typing msoShape16pointStar, you will get the error in Figure 9.1, and the line with the error will turn red. In this case, we are missing the close parenthesis, so we can add it:

```
Sub AddStar()
    ActivePresentation.SlideShowWindow.View.Slide.Shapes.AddShape _
        (msoShape16pointStar)
End Sub
```

Now when you hit Enter, the line doesn't turn red. Does that mean that it works? No, it does not. But we're ready to try it out to see if it works.

Create a button and tie it to the procedure AddStar. Go to Slide Show View and click on your button. No news is bad news. The VBA Editor (or more accurately, the VBA compiler) couldn't find anything wrong as you typed, but when VBA tried to run the procedure, it couldn't figure it out, so it just gave up.

Unfortunately, we don't have any more clues as to what is wrong. However, since we are adding a shape, we might remember that we need to tell VBA where the shape should go and how big it should be:

```
Sub AddStar()
    ActivePresentation.SlideShowWindow.View.Slide.Shapes.AddShape _
        (msoShape16pointStar, 100, 100, 100, 100)
End Sub
```

We have told VBA that we want our shape to be 100 pixels from the left of the screen, 100 pixels from the top of the screen, 100 pixels wide, and 100 pixels tall. This should fully define our shape. Hit Enter and now VBA starts to complain again with the error in Figure 9.2.

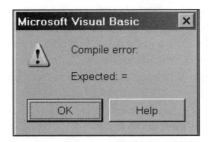

Figure 9.2. Typical Compile Error

Now, VBA thinks we are missing an equals sign. This is a good example of a cryptic message that can be a bit deceiving. In fact, we are missing an equals sign, but simply adding an equals sign (like we added a parenthesis earlier) won't do the trick. The problem here (as is often the problem when VBA complains about a missing equals sign) is that we have created an object, and when VBA creates an object, it wants to put that object in a variable (whether or not we ever want to do anything with that object again). Thus, we need to set a variable to point to the new object (using Set because it is an object):

```
Sub AddStar()
   Set myShape = _
      ActivePresentation.SlideShowWindow.View.Slide.Shapes.AddShape _
      (msoShape16pointStar, 100, 100, 100, 100)
End Sub
```

Now, we are in good shape! If you hit Enter, nothing will turn red, but we won't know if it works until we try it. Go back to PowerPoint, go to Slide Show View, and click on your button. If all goes well, you will now have a new shape on your slide.

Of course, if you click on the button a second time, nothing will happen. Or, it will appear that nothing happens. That is because you will create another shape on top of the first shape. If you go back into Edit View in PowerPoint, you can see that you have two shapes by dragging one of the shapes out of the way.

I'm Not Seeing Red, But I'm Seeing Red

The above example was fairly simple. It was one line, so we knew where the problem was; it had to be in that line. Many of your procedures will be more complicated. If you have a procedure with two or three or ten or twenty lines, you won't know where the problem is. One small error in the middle of a procedure might cause your button to do nothing. You should be able to catch the errors that the VBA Editor turns red because they will be red, but the ones that don't turn red are harder to find.

Now we need some way to figure out which line is the problem for those errors that don't turn red. While VBA has some tools to help you with debugging, these tools are not always the best choice. That is because of the distinction between Slide Show View and Edit View. When you are in the VBA Editor, PowerPoint is generally sitting in Edit View. Remember that most of our procedures are made to work in Slide Show View (anything that starts with ActivePresentation.SlideShowWindow is only going to work in Slide Show View).

To solve this problem, you can use MsgBox. MsgBox is a simple (read that as "hard to mess up") command that pops up a message. Add a few MsgBox commands to your code with informative messages that tell you what you are expecting and where you are in the code. For example, you might put a MsgBox at the beginning of the procedure:

```
MsgBox("Entering the procedure AddStar.")
```

When you run the procedure, if you don't even get a message that pops up to say, "Entering the procedure AddStar," you know the problem probably is not in the procedure (unless it is in the Dim statements in the procedure because the first `MsgBox` has to come after the procedure's `Dim` statements). It could be that you linked your button to the wrong procedure or, in a more complicated script, it could be that the problem is in another procedure that calls this one. If you get the message, you know you have gotten into the procedure. Now, you can add some more `MsgBox` commands to try to locate the problem. For example:

```
Sub AddStar()
   Dim myShape As Shape

   MsgBox ("Entering the procedure AddStar.")
   Set myShape = _
      ActivePresentation.SlideShowWindow.View.Slide.Shapes.AddShape _
      (msoShape16pointStar, 100, 100, 100, 100)
   MsgBox ("I just added the shape, and I'm about to add some text.")
   myShape.TextFrame.TextRange.Text = "Good job!"
   MsgBox ("I just added some text, and I'm about to change the color.")
   mShape.Fill.ForeColor.RGB = vbBlue
   MsgBox ("Color is changed; now I'll change the size.")
   myShape.Height = 200
   myShape.Width = 200
   MsgBox ("I am about to leave AddStar.")
End Sub
```

Try running the above procedure. See if you can find the error. As you run the procedure, you should get the messages:

- Entering the procedure AddStar.

- I just added the shape, and I'm about to add some text.

- I just added some text, and I'm about to change the color.

But that will be it. You will know that the problem is probably in the following line. If you look closely, you will see that the line has a small typo; it uses `mShape` instead of `myShape`. Once the problem is fixed, try it out again. If it works, you can delete all the `MsgBox` lines.

You can also use a `MsgBox` to tell you what is in a variable. For example, if something is wrong with the scoring in a quiz, you might want to use the following line at various places to get updates about what the computer thinks the score is:

```
MsgBox ("The value of numCorrect is " & numCorrect)
```

This will work most of the time. Unfortunately, certain kinds of errors will not turn red and will not allow the procedure to run at all (for example, instead of misspelling `myShape`, try misspelling `RGB`). These are harder to find and are a good reason to use some tricks to prevent errors in the first place (see "An Ounce of Prevention").

Commenting Out

Because the MsgBox method, in the previous section, works sometimes and doesn't work other times, you might need another *old programmer's trick* to find your error: commenting out. Remember that everything on a VBA line after a single quote is ignored; that is, it is a comment. You can put a single quote at the beginning of a line and that entire line will be ignored. This is better than deleting the line because you still have the code there, and you can get it to run again by deleting the single quote. Note that the VBA Editor turns comments green, so if you have anything that is green in your code, it is ignored by VBA.

```
Sub AddStar()
   Dim myShape As Shape

   MsgBox ("Entering the procedure AddStar.")
   Set myShape = _
      ActivePresentation.SlideShowWindow.View.Slide.Shapes.AddShape _
      (mso16pointStar, 100, 100, 100, 100)
   MsgBox ("I just added the shape, and I'm about to add some text.")
   myShape.TextFrame.TextRange.Text = "Good job!"
   MsgBox ("I just added some text, and I'm about to change the color.")
   myShape.Fill.ForeColor.RGB = vbBlue
   MsgBox ("Color is changed; now I'll change the size.")
   myShape.Height = 200
   myShape.Width = 200
   MsgBox ("I am about to leave AddStar.")
End Sub
```

The above procedure is similar to the one earlier, except there is a different error. If you try running the procedure with this error, nothing will happen. You won't even get "Entering the procedure AddStar." That means that it is time to comment out some lines to try to track down the problem. Since nothing can work until the shape is created, you probably want to start with the line after Set myShape . . . .

```
Sub AddStar()
   Dim myShape As Shape

   MsgBox ("Entering the procedure AddStar")
   Set myShape = _
      ActivePresentation.SlideShowWindow.View.Slide.Shapes.AddShape _
      (mso16pointStar, 100, 100, 100, 100)
   'MsgBox ("I just added the shape, and I'm about to add some text.")
   'myShape.TextFrame.TextRange.Text = "Good job!"
   'MsgBox ("I just added some text, and I'm about to change the color.")
   'myShape.Fill.ForeColor.RGB = vbBlue
   'MsgBox ("Color is changed; now I'll change the size.")
   'myShape.Height = 200
   'myShape.Width = 200
   'MsgBox ("I am about to leave AddStar.")
End Sub
```

You'll notice that all the lines after the `Set myShape` (except `End Sub`) line are green in the VBA Editor. These lines will not run. As far as VBA is concerned, they are not even there.

Try running the procedure with all the comments. If it works, start removing the comments (just the single quotes, not the whole lines) from the line below `Set myShape`. Run it again. If it works, remove the comment from the next line and run it again. Keep removing one comment and running it again until it stops working. When it stops working, you have found the problem line. It must be the last line from which you removed the comment. If you have removed all the comments and it still doesn't work, then the problem is probably the `Dim` statement or the `Set myShape` line.

If you go through this exercise, you'll find that the problem is with the `Set myShape` line. `mso16PointStar` should be `msoShape16PointStar`. Often the parameters of procedures are the kinds of errors that will cause a procedure to not work at all, rather than work until it reaches an error. But the best way to eliminate errors is to practice some prevention techniques. They won't prevent all errors, but they will cut down on errors.

Compiling Your Code

Sometimes your code will not work, and you won't know why. You might have tried all the techniques above, but you still can't find the bug. There is one more technique that sometimes gives more information: compiling your code.

Certain kinds of errors are *run time errors*. These happen when your code is running. The computer doesn't know that there is a bug until it tries to run the code. Other kinds of errors are *compile errors*. These are errors in which the computer can see a problem before you run the code. Errors that turn red are one type of compile error, generally errors that affect one specific line of code. Other errors do not turn red, but they make all the code stop working.

You can find compile errors by choosing "Compile VBAProject" from the Debug menu in the VBA Editor. This will look over your code for any errors that the computer can catch before your code is run.

If you get a message that includes "Compile error," you will probably get some useful information about what is wrong. It will probably highlight where the problem is in your code and describe the problem. For example, the error "Argument not optional" tells you that you are missing an argument for a procedure or method. And you will know which procedure or method is missing the argument because it will be highlighted. If you have more than one compile error, then you will have to do this again because the compiler stops on the first error it finds. Fix the first error and compile your project again to see if there are any more errors.

Debugger

The VBA Editor comes with a debugger. In some cases, this will be useful, but it will not work well for most of our code. The debugger lets you set break-points to stop your code at certain points as it runs. Unfortunately, this does not work well for code that runs in Slide Show View, so it is not useful for most of our purposes.

An Ounce of Prevention

As you write your code, you can use several techniques to help you catch bugs as you type. These techniques will not prevent all bugs, but they will cut down on the number you have to find later. If you are perfect and never make mistakes, these techniques won't affect anything. The techniques are for human eyes; the computer will be able to run your code without them. But for those of us who are not perfect, our human eyes need all the help we can get to catch bugs or prevent them from happening.

Capitalization

You might have looked at some of the examples and wondered why certain things were capitalized in certain ways. Some of it is part of the technique to prevent bugs, and some of it is forced upon you by VBA. There are five kinds of things you can type into the VBA Editor:

1. Comments
2. Text between quotes
3. Variable names
4. Procedure names
5. VBA stuff (built-in function names, procedure names, object names, etc.)

Comments can be capitalized any way that you like because they are for you to read. Pay close attention to capitalization of text between quotes because that will usually be displayed for your students, but for the purposes of debugging, it doesn't matter how you capitalize it. Capitalization of the last three items can be important for debugging.

In this book, I have used the following convention: Variable names begin with a lowercase letter; and procedure names begin with an uppercase letter. Furthermore, since variable names and procedure names cannot contain spaces, any new word in the name begins with an uppercase letter. This is a convention, a technique, a trick. I could have used `yourName` instead of `YourName` and `UserName` instead of `userName`. It would have worked fine. However, if you use this convention, you can look at your code and always tell whether a name refers to a variable or a procedure by looking at the capitalization. Capitalizing the first letter of each subsequent word in a variable or procedure name simply helps you read it more easily. You want to be able to read the names because you picked names that make sense to you.

You should be able to tell immediately that the following are variables, and you probably even have a reasonable idea of what information they hold: `myShape`, `numCorrect`, `userName`, `printableSlide`. You should be able to tell immediately that the following are procedures: `YourName`, `RightAnswer`, `AddStar`.

For the VBA stuff, you don't have a choice about capitalization. Most VBA stuff will be capitalized for you, no matter how you type it. This is a good thing that can help prevent bugs.

Don't Capitalize to Prevent Bugs

While you are writing your scripts, the VBA Editor tries to be helpful. You might find this annoying at times, but many of its helpful features can prevent future problems.

The VBA Editor will automatically adjust your capitalization for you. This might seem excessively meticulous, but you can use it to catch typing mistakes. You'll notice that built-in procedures and commands (such as `MsgBox` and `Dim`) all start with capitals. The only times you should capitalize words yourself are in `Dim` statements (declaring variables), `Sub` statements (at the beginning of procedures), and inside quotes.

If you follow the capitalization convention, after you have declared a variable with a `Dim` statement, always type it in lowercase. And after you write a procedure and capitalize it properly in the `Sub` statement, if you call the procedure from another procedure, you can type its name in lowercase. Not only is it easier to type in lowercase, it will help you catch mistakes.

After you type a line and hit Enter (or click somewhere else in your script), the VBA Editor will automatically adjust the capitalization. For example, type the following:

```
activepresentation.slideshowwindow.view.next
```

When you hit Enter, the VBA Editor will change it to:

```
ActivePresentation.SlideShowWindow.View.Next
```

The power of this is apparent when you type something wrong. If you left out a "t" in `ActivePresentation`, for example, that would not be capitalized. For example, type the following:

```
activepresenation.slideshowwindow.view.next
```

When you hit Enter, it changes to:

```
activepresenation.SlideShowWindow.View.Next
```

The fact that `activepresenation` did not change in capitalization is a tip-off that something is wrong.

This also works for any variables that you have declared and procedures you have written. The VBA Editor gets the capitalization that you want to use from the `Dim` statement and the `Sub` statement (that's why you have to type with proper capitalization in the `Dim` and `Sub` statements) and automatically adjusts the capitalization as you type the variable or procedure name in the future. If the capitalization is not automatically adjusted for you, you have either misspelled the name of the variable or procedure or have forgotten to declare the variable.

Misspelling the name of a variable or procedure gives the same results as misspelling a keyword: The capitalization will not be changed by the VBA Editor. For example, type the following:

```
Dim userName As String
Sub YourName()
    usernam = InputBox(prompt:="Type your name")
End Sub
```

Because `userName` is misspelled as `usernam`, the n did not get capitalized.

Indenting

You might have noticed that throughout the text, code examples were indented in a very specific way. Indenting helps you read the code. The computer will understand your code just fine without indenting, but you are more likely to make mistakes without it. "Conditionals" in Chapter 8 discussed indenting briefly because indenting is very helpful for reading `If` statements. It is also helpful for reading loops. The more complex the code, the more helpful indenting is.

You can use your own style for indenting, but whatever you decide, you should stick with it. The easiest way to indent in the VBA Editor is to use the Tab key. When you hit Tab at the beginning of a line, the line will be indented once. When you hit Enter to go to the next line, the next line will be indented at the same level. If you don't want it indented, simply hit the Backspace key (Delete on a Macintosh) or hold down the Shift key and hit Tab (shift-Tab). If you have a block of lines that you want to indent, you can highlight them and hit Tab (or shift-Tab if you want to un-indent them).

In this book, I have indented three kinds of statements:

1. Everything between a `Sub` and an `End Sub` is indented one level.

2. Everything that is part of a block is indented. This includes parts of an `If` block (such as everything between an `If` and `ElseIf` or everything

between an `ElseIf` and the next `ElseIf` or everything between an `Else` and an `End If`). This also includes loops (such as everything between a `For` and `Next` or everything between a `While` and `Wend`).

3. Lines that are continued from the previous line (where the previous line ends with an underscore) are indented.

Indenting helps you see that something is a part of something else: A group of lines is part of the `Sub`, a group of lines is part of the `ElseIf` portion of an `If` block, a continued line is a part of the previous line, etc. Look at the following example:

```
Sub NestedIf()
If gradeNum > 90 Then
MsgBox ("Great job. You got an A.")
If gradeNum = 100 Then
MsgBox ("You are perfect.")
End If
ElseIf gradeNum > 80 Then
MsgBox ("Good work. B is a very good grade.")
ElseIf gradeNum > 70 Then
MsgBox ("Not bad. C is still passing.")
If gradeNum < 72 Then
MsgBox ("That was close. You were lucky to get a C.")
End If
Else
MsgBox ("You can do better than this.")
End If
If gradNum > 70 Then
MsgBox ("You have passed this class.")
End If
End Sub
```

You might be able to understand this code, but without indenting, it is hard to tell which `End If` goes with which `If` and under what circumstances each line will get executed. This is much easier to understand when everything is indented:

```
Sub NestedIf()
   If gradeNum > 90 Then
      MsgBox ("Great job. You got an A.")
      If gradeNum = 100 Then
         MsgBox ("You are perfect.")
      End If
   ElseIf gradeNum > 80 Then
      MsgBox ("Good work. B is a very good grade.")
   ElseIf gradeNum > 70 Then
      MsgBox ("Not bad. C is still passing.")
      If gradeNum < 72 Then
         MsgBox ("That was close. You were lucky to get a C.")
      End If
   Else
      MsgBox ("You can do better than this.")
   End If
   If gradNum > 70 Then
      MsgBox ("You have passed this class.")
   End If
End Sub
```

Each part that is indented is now clearly part of the line before it. It is easiest to indent and un-indent as you go because as you type your code, you know what you mean.

Hints from the VBA Editor

On a Windows computer, the VBA Editor often tries to give you helpful suggestions. You might have noticed that when you type a dot, sometimes a box pops up with possibilities for what to type next. See Figure 9.3 for an example.

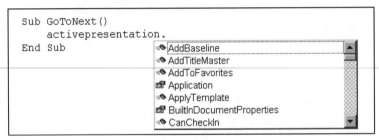

Figure 9.3. Auto-Complete Suggestions from the VBA Editor

In this case the scrollable window gives you a list of all the things you can type after `ActivePresentation`. You can choose from the list by double-clicking on any item, or you can start typing. As you type, the window highlights the first thing in the list (in alphabetical order) that matches what you type. If nothing is highlighted, you have typed something wrong. Generally, that list is all that is available to type. If the list of choices has gone away, you can delete the line back to the dot; when you type the dot again, the list will come back.

In addition, in Windows the VBA Editor will make some suggestions for parameters for procedures. For example, if you type

```
activepresentation.slideshowwindow.view.gotoslide(
```

the VBA editor will give you some hints about what you can type next, specifically what parameters the `GotoSlide` method wants (see Figure 9.4).

```
Sub GoToNext()
    activepresentation.slideshowwindow.view.gotoslide(
End Sub         GotoSlide(Index As Long, [ResetSlide As MsoTriState = msoTrue])
```

Figure 9.4. VBA Editor Suggests Parameters for the GotoSlide Method

The little box has a lot of details that will help you. First, you can see that there are two possible parameters separated by commas: `Index` and `ResetSlide`. Although the box does not tell you what the parameters are for, it does tell you what kind of information they need. In this case, `Index` is a `Long` variable (that's a kind of integer). You can probably figure out that it is the slide number of the slide to go to. `ResetSlide` is an `MsoTriState` variable (which is usually just a `True` or `False` value).

You should also notice that `Index` is not in square brackets, but `ResetSlide` is. This tells us that `Index` is required and `ResetSlide` is not. That is, you have to tell `GotoSlide` which slide to go to, but you don't have to tell it whether or not to reset (the `ResetSlide` tells it whether or not to reset the animation effects on the slide; i.e., leave them in their final state or put them back at the beginning state). Also, notice that `ResetSlide` has a default value. That is, if you don't include a value for `ResetSlide`, it will assume you wanted `msoTrue` (which is basically the same as `True`), which means that the slide will be reset. Finally, you will notice that `Index` is in bold. That means that the next thing I type will be the value used for `Index`. If I type a number and then a comma, `ResetSlide` will become bold, meaning that the next value I type will be the value for `ResetSlide`. If you type parameters in order, you can just type the values as in the following:

```
ActivePresentation.SlideShowWindow.View.GotoSlide(5,True)
```

If you don't type them in order, you can use the parameter name, followed by colon equals sign (: =), followed by the value, as in the following:

```
ActivePresentation.SlideShowWindow.View.GotoSlide(ResetSlide:=True, _
    Index:=5)
```

This is very helpful for a couple of reasons. First, you don't always have to look up which parameters are needed. For example, when adding a shape, I can never remember which comes first and second: `Top` and `Left` or `Width` and `Height`. I don't need to remember because VBA will tell me, as in Figure 9.5.

```
Sub AddShape()
    Dim myShape

    Set myShape = _
        ActivePresentation.SlideShowWindow.View.Slide.Shapes. _
        AddShape(
End Sub      AddShape(Type As MsoAutoShapeType, Left As Single, Top As Single, Width As Single, Height As
            Single) As Shape
```

Figure 9.5. VBA Editor Suggests Parameters for the AddShape Method

Second, you always know what the procedure expects. If you leave off any required parameters (such as forgetting to specify `Width` and `Height`), it won't work.

VBA Help

While Windows versions of the VBA Editor are better at suggesting things as you type, Macintosh versions have help that is a bit easier to use. In either version of VBA, you can choose one of the selections from the Help menu to search for a keyword. In the Macintosh version, you can highlight a keyword, object, or method in your code and hit the Help key on your keyboard. This will bring up help that is directly related to what you are trying to do.

When you are using help, you can get all the information that pops up on your screen when you type open parenthesis and VBA suggests parameters. You should also check out the examples to help you understand what you are doing better.

Common Bugs

Everyone makes mistakes, and everyone makes their own mistakes. However, a few mistakes are fairly common. If you can't track down a bug, you might look for some of these things. The bugs listed below are particularly tricky to find because they are not a problem with a specific procedure. If one procedure is not working at all or is giving the wrong results, you can usually find the bug if you stare at that procedure long enough (or use some of the above techniques to track it down). However, the following bugs cause problems for procedures that are completely correct and might have been working a minute earlier. No matter how long you stare at a procedure, you won't find the bug if it is caused by something outside the procedure.

Multiple Modules

You were warned early in this book that you should have only one module for each presentation. If you have gotten this far in the book, you have probably heeded that warning. However, some people get confused and add a second module. Some things will work with more than one module, and some things won't. Check the Project window to be sure that you have only one module. If you can't remember how to check the modules in your Project window, look back at Chapter 4 in "Help! I've Lost My Windows."

Usually, when you add one module, it will be named "Module1." However, if you played around with modules or accidentally deleted a module, your module might be "Module2" or "Module3." That is OK as long as there is only one module, whatever it is named. If you have put code in more than one module, use cut and paste to move all the code into one module. If you had Dim statements at the top of each module, be sure you put them all together at the top of your one module and remove any duplicates.

Duplicate Variables

When we declare our variables at the beginning of a module, we create a box to put information in, and we give that box a name. What if two boxes have the same name? That would be a problem, and VBA would not know what to do. In fact, nothing in your module would work at all. You could have buttons tied to procedures that have nothing to do with the variable that is declared twice, but they would not work. Nothing would work.

You might have this problem if you are combining two examples or have a long list of variables that you declare at the beginning of your module, and you forgot you already declared a variable. If none of your VBA works, check the variable declarations at the beginning of the module and delete any duplicate Dim statements.

Duplicate Procedures

Just like VBA doesn't know what to do when you have two variables with the same name, it doesn't know what to do when you have two procedures with the same name. You might have been playing around with the examples in this book and accidentally wrote two YourName procedures. They might be exactly the same or different, but if they have the same name, nothing will work. Figure out which procedure does what you want and delete the duplicate. Or, if the two procedures are really supposed to be doing different things, give one of them a different name. You might also want to add a comment to explain what each procedure does.

> Note that variables and procedures are not allowed to have the same name. If you give a procedure the same name as a variable, it will not work.

Extra End Sub

The VBA Editor is nice. It never requires you to type End Sub. When you hit the Enter key after typing a Sub line, the editor automatically types the End Sub. Most of the time, this is a good thing. Occasionally, it is not, such as when it leads to your code having too many End Sub lines. Since you don't type the End Sub lines, it is easy for extra ones to be added to your code.

If your code stops working, check for extra End Sub lines. They might be at the end of the module or at the end of a procedure. Usually they're in a place that is not showing on your screen, so you'll have to scroll to see them. Delete the extra End Sub, and your code might work again.

The Forgotten `Dim`

In some cases you don't need to declare variables, but if you want a variable to remember something later, you must declare it at the beginning of the module. It is easy to forget to do this. If, for example, you forget to declare `userName`, then `YourName` will work perfectly fine asking for a name and storing it in `userName`, but once `YourName` is finished, `userName` is forgotten.

If you have forgotten to declare a variable, like `userName`, you might have a perfectly good `YourName` procedure and a perfectly good `DoingWell` procedure, but when `DoingWell` is run, it says "Good job," not "Good job, Ada." If your presentation seems to be forgetful, check your `Dim` statements to be sure that you have declared all your variables at the beginning of the module.

Final Word on Debugging and Error Prevention

The final word on debugging and error prevention is to test what you have done. If you can, test each procedure and/or button right away, so you can fix any problems before you have too much code with too many problems to deal with. But most important, test. You can't fix a bug that you don't find. And believe me, your students will find the bugs. Try clicking on buttons that you didn't want the students to click on, clicking on wrong answers, and typing unexpected things. Your students will, and your presentation needs to be prepared for that.

Debugging and error prevention is more of an art form than a science. You will develop your own techniques the more comfortable you get. But debugging and error prevention is very important because you *will* have bugs (fewer if you use the error prevention techniques), and you will need to correct them.

Conclusion

In this chapter you learned about ways to find bugs, how to fix bugs, and how to prevent bugs. Now that you have learned a great many VBA tricks and how to make your code work (or fix it when it doesn't), you are ready to create your own projects as well as create templates for your students' projects. The next chapter talks about the idea of creating templates that provide the framework of a project for your students so they can fill in the content.

Exercises to Try

✍ The following code is not indented. What will happen if Ella types 5? What will happen if anyone else types 5? What will happen if Ella types 10? What will happen if anyone else types 10? Try to figure it out without running the code. Type it into the VBA Editor and indent it properly; see if you come up with a different answer now that it is indented. Run the code to see if you got the right answer.

```
Sub HowDoYouFeel()
Dim score As Integer
Dim userName As String
userName = InputBox("What is your name?")
score = InputBox("On a scale of 1 to 10, how do you feel?")
If score > 5 Then
If score > 7 Then
If score > 9 Then
If userName = "Ella" Then
If score > 10 Then
MsgBox ("That's amazing")
Else
MsgBox ("That's perfect")
End If
ElseIf score < 6 Then
MsgBox ("That's middling")
Else
MsgBox ("You're perfect.")
End If
ElseIf score = 5 Then
MsgBox ("Are you middling?")
Else
MsgBox ("Are you above average?")
End If
ElseIf score = 5 Then
MsgBox ("Right in the middle")
Else
MsgBox ("That's good")
End If
Else
MsgBox ("Not too good.")
End If
End Sub
```

✎ The following is the entire contents of a module. It contains four bugs. Try to find all four by typing the code into the VBA Editor and using the debugging and error prevention methods in this chapter.

```
Sub YourName()
userName = InputBox("What is your name?")
End Sub
End Sub
Sub BadProcedure()
YorName
If userName = "Ella" Then
MsgBox ("Hello, big girl.")
ElseIf userName = "Ada"
MsgBox ("Hello, little girl.")
Else
MsgBox ("Hello, " & userName)
End If
End Sub
```

10

Templates

Introduction

In Chapter 9 you learned the last technical tricks presented in this book and developed a bag of tricks to help you fix any problems that you might encounter. Now you are ready to embark on using all the tricks you have learned to make powerful interactive projects. However, your students might not be ready to make their own powerful interactive projects. This chapter describes templates, a tool you can use to do the technical and design work for your students, allowing them to concentrate on the content. With a template, you can use all the VBA features that you want, and your students can use all those VBA features without even knowing how to open the VBA Editor. This chapter describes templates and provides several examples, including a sophisticated example that asks the user for information and adds a slide with that information.

Vocabulary

- Design Template (.pot) File   • Template

What Are Templates?

Previous chapters emphasized the use of multimedia projects that are created by the educator. As you have read this book and worked through the examples, I hope you have gotten several ideas for projects that you want to create for your students. A more powerful use of multimedia is to have students create their own projects. Many studies have shown the positive educational impact of students designing their own multimedia projects. See, for example, Liu and Hsiao (2001), Liu and Rutledge (1997), or Lehrer, Erickson, and Connell (1994). While this can be a powerful educational opportunity, it also can be impractical for a number of reasons, not the least of which are that it is very time-consuming and that your students might lack the technical skills to be successful.

Have no fear. Your students can still get many of the benefits of what you have learned in this book without having to learn it all (or any of it) themselves. That is where templates come in. If you design a project from scratch, you have to decide on the appropriate media, appropriate kinds of information, and appropriate organization for your project. In addition, you have to develop the project (including preparing the media, the PowerPoint slides, the VBA, etc.). A template allows you to create some of these things for your students. Templates have been used to facilitate multimedia creation by professional designers; see, for example, O'Connor (1991). Agnew, Kellerman, and Meyer discusses the use of templates with students: "The primary purpose of giving students a template for their early projects is to allow them to concentrate most of their attention on achieving academic objectives" (1996, p. 250).

Something as simple as a PowerPoint project about an animal can use a template. You could tell your students that the presentation should contain four slides: a title slide, a slide about the animal's habitat with a picture of the animal, a slide about what the animal eats, and a slide for citing resources. Those simple instructions are a rudimentary template. You have designed the organization of the project for the students.

However, you might go further and actually create the slides for them, giving your students directions about how to fill in the picture and the text. See Figure 10.1 for an example.

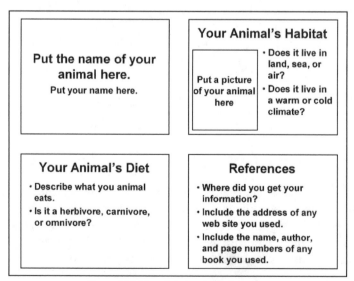

Figure 10.1. Template for Animal Project

Although this is not a complex project, it might be a good one for second graders, for example, who are first being introduced to PowerPoint. This project does not require VBA or hyperlinks or animations or anything but the most basic features of PowerPoint. For a class of students who are new to PowerPoint, by getting them started you can save them hours of computer work and allow them to concentrate on the content.

As projects become more complex, templates become more powerful. You might want to introduce your students slowly to advanced features of PowerPoint, or you might not want to introduce them to some features at all. But you might want them to take full advantage of these features right away.

In Chapter 8 we saw examples of projects that easily can be turned into templates. You might want your students to write quizzes with all the features of VBA that we discussed, but you might not want them to have to deal with VBA. Using the examples from Chapter 8, you can set up a template with no questions or a fake question and give your students instructions about how to add slides and tie the buttons to the appropriate procedures. For the multiple-choice examples, they don't need to change the VBA code at all.

As another template example, chapter 7 of Agnew, Kellerman, and Meyer (1996) discusses a current events project. In this project, each student or group of students creates a single slide about a current event. The slide contains a brief paragraph about the event and a button for the citation and photograph of the event. This project could be done as a template in which the teacher creates all the parts of the project and the students simply add the pictures, citations, and news summaries. In the end, all the slides are put together to form a class collection of current events.

Many topics would work well in a template format. Projects that work especially well are ones in which you would like the students to include a fixed body of information, and each student or group includes the same kind of information about a different topic. For example, school clubs, U.S. presidents, countries in Europe, Spanish verbs, and state flags are all topics that lend themselves well to templates.

Saving Your Template

When you create a template in PowerPoint, you can save it as a regular PowerPoint presentation or as a Design Template. If you save it as a regular PowerPoint presentation, you can have your students edit it, and you have to be sure they choose "Save As" from the File menu to save it under a new name. If they choose "Save," it might overwrite the original file and lose the template.

If you save your template as a Design Template, when students double-click on the file to open it, they will be taken to a new presentation that is based on the template. When they save this file, they will be asked to choose a new name and location for the presentation, so it will not overwrite the original template.

To save your presentation as a Design Template, you will have to pay attention to the "Save as type." If you choose, "Design Template" as your file type, it will create a .pot file (see Figure 10.2).

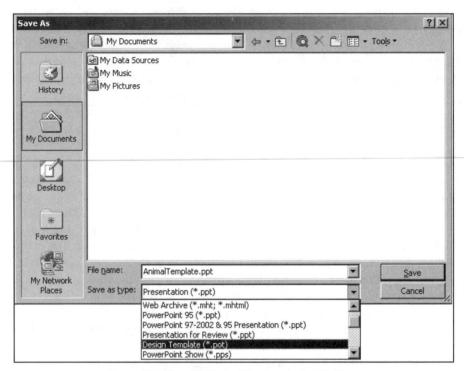

Figure 10.2. Choosing Design Template As the File Type

If you save a file as a Design Template, you can edit the template (rather than a project based on the template) by opening the project from within PowerPoint. That is, start PowerPoint and choose "Open" from the File menu to open it.

Once you have created a template, either as a .pot file or as a regular PowerPoint presentation, you might want to set it to be "Read-only." To do this, quit out of PowerPoint and click once on the file to select it. If you are in Windows, choose "Properties" from the File menu and check the box labeled "Read-only." If you are on a Macintosh, choose "Get Info" from the File menu and check the box labeled "Locked." This will prevent the template from being changed accidentally.

The Pick-A-Partner Template Project

In my Multimedia Design in the Classroom class, I encourage students to form groups to complete their final projects. While this could be done in a number of ways (with or without technology), I also want to be sure my students are up to speed on the traditional features of PowerPoint at the beginning of class. To that end, I have them fill in a PowerPoint template. The template gives my students a chance to brush up on their traditional PowerPoint skills and view the power of VBA without needing to know any VBA. In a less technically oriented class, a similar project could be used for the same purposes. If you plan to use PowerPoint for later projects, you can use a project like this one to introduce your students to some of the features of PowerPoint.

This project is a twist on a common exercise to introduce PowerPoint in which students fill in information about themselves. In my class, this information is specifically related to what they might want to do with their final projects. Figure 10.3 shows the slides for the template.

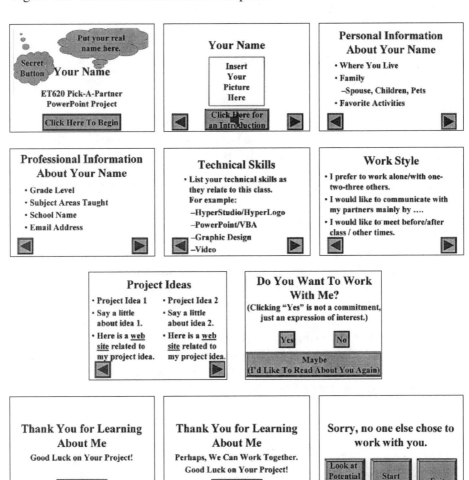

Figure 10.3. Slides for Pick-A-Partner Template

In the template, clouds represent instructions to the students who will be filling in the content. The students are told to follow the instructions in the clouds and delete the clouds when they are done. In Figure 10.3, the cloud instructions are only shown on the first slide, but I generally include them on all slides.

Once all students fill in the content for their presentations, students rotate around the room looking at each others' presentations. When they reach the "Do You Want To Work With Me?" slide, if they choose "Yes," they are asked for a name, an e-mail address, and a project idea.

Most of the project uses traditional PowerPoint features. The first seven slides use features such as text, sound, pictures, buttons, and hyperlinks. VBA is used in the first slide, the eighth slide, and the last slide to do the following:

- Some minor navigation tricks were achieved with VBA.

- Users are asked to input name, e-mail address, and project ideas.

- A new slide is created with the information the user inputs and a button to advance to the next slide.

- A button is used to navigate to a particular slide number (not a named slide as is done with standard PowerPoint) so it can reach the slide that was created with VBA.

Figure 10.4 shows the complete code for this project. Remember that, because this is a template, my students do not type any of this code. They simply fill in the content in the first seven slides.

On the first slide, the secret button (the invisible button in the upper left corner) is tied to the procedure GoToPartners. This procedure goes to the eleventh slide. Normally, this could be done with a traditional hyperlink, but in this case, the eleventh slide is going to be created with VBA. A traditional hyperlink cannot link to a slide that does not yet exist. On the last slide, the "Look at Potential Partners Again" button also is tied to GoToPartners for the same reason.

The only other button that uses VBA is the "Yes" button on the eighth slide. When users decide they want to work with you, they click on this button to initiate a series of events. This button is tied to the WorkTogether procedure, which controls this series of events.

```vba
Dim userName As String
Dim userEmail As String
Dim userIdea As String
Sub WorkTogether()
    GetNameEmailIdea
    GoToWorkTogether
    AddWorkTogetherSlide
    Save
End Sub
Sub YourName()
    Dim done As Boolean
    done = False
    While Not done
        userName = InputBox(prompt:="Type your name", _
            Title:="Name")
        If userName = "" Then done = False Else done = True
    Wend
End Sub
Sub YourEmail()
    Dim done As Boolean
    done = False
    While Not done
        userEmail = InputBox(prompt:="Type your Email Address", _
            Title:="Email")
        If userEmail = "" Then done = False Else done = True
    Wend
End Sub
Sub YourIdea()
    userIdea = InputBox(prompt:="Type one project idea (optional)", _
        Title:="Idea")
End Sub
Sub GetNameEmailIdea()
    YourName
    YourEmail
    YourIdea
End Sub
Sub GoToWorkTogether()
    ActivePresentation.SlideShowWindow.View.GotoSlide (10)
End Sub
Sub Save()
    ActivePresentation.Save
End Sub
Sub AddNextSlideButton(index As Long)
    Dim myShape As Shape
    Set myShape = ActivePresentation.Slides(index).Shapes _
        .AddShape(msoShapeActionButtonForwardorNext, 612#, 456#, 82.12, 82.12)
    With myShape.ActionSettings(ppMouseClick)
        .Action = ppActionNextSlide
        .SoundEffect.Type = ppSoundNone
        .AnimateAction = msoTrue
    End With
    With myShape
        .Fill.ForeColor.SchemeColor = ppAccent1
        .Fill.Visible = msoTrue
        .Fill.Solid
        .Line.ForeColor.RGB = RGB(255, 255, 255)
        .Line.Visible = msoTrue
    End With
End Sub
Sub AddWorkTogetherSlide()
    ActivePresentation.Slides.Add index:=11, Layout:=ppLayoutText
    With ActivePresentation.Slides(11)
        .Shapes(1).TextFrame.TextRange.Text = userName & " is interested in working with you."
        .Shapes(2).TextFrame.TextRange.Text = "Email: " & userEmail
        With .Shapes(2).TextFrame.TextRange
            If userIdea = "" Then .Text = .Text & Chr$(13) & "No ideas entered" _
                Else .Text = .Text & Chr$(13) & "An idea to ponder: " & userIdea
        End With
    End With
    AddNextSlideButton (11)
End Sub
Sub GoToPartners()
    ActivePresentation.SlideShowWindow.View.GotoSlide (11)
End Sub
```

Figure 10.4. Pick-A-Partner VBA Code

The `WorkTogether` procedure calls all the procedures needed to make everything happen. When I took my first computer course, the instructor told us to think about what we wanted our program to do and write a top-level procedure to call other procedures to do it. Then, he suggested that you have finished something important and you should go have a beer. That is what the `WorkTogether` procedure does. Go have a beer (if you are of legal drinking age, not driving, not pregnant, etc.)! This procedure does all of the following:

- It asks the user to input a name, e-mail address, and project idea (`GetNameEmailIdea`).

- It jumps to the tenth slide thanking the user for wanting to work with you (`GoToWorkTogether`).

- It creates a new slide that contains the name, e-mail, address, and project idea (`AddWorkTogetherSlide`),

- It saves the presentation so the newly added slide becomes part of the presentation (`Save`),

The procedures `YourName`, `YourEmail`, and `YourIdea` are all variations of the `YourName` procedure from earlier chapters. Although any version of `YourName` will work, `YourName` and `YourEmail` use a version that forces the user to type something. Because giving a project idea is optional, `YourIdea` uses a version that does not require the user to type anything. The name, e-mail address, and project idea are stored in the variables `userName`, `userEmail`, and `userIdea` respectively. At the appropriate time, all three of these procedures are called in succession by the `GetNameEmailIdea` procedure, which simply calls each of these procedures in turn. However, `GetNameEmailIdea` is not tied directly to any buttons because when users press the button to say they want to be your partner, all the magic happens (coordinated by the `WorkTogether` procedure), not just the input part.

The `GoToWorkTogether` procedure is simply a navigational procedure that goes to the tenth slide because that is the slide that contains the message "Thank You For Learning About Me. Perhaps We Can Work Together." This, by itself, could easily be done with traditional PowerPoint actions, but this is one of many things that happens when a single button is pressed; that is, it is part of all the things that `WorkTogether` does.

The procedure `Save` simply saves the presentation (as described in Chapter 8). This is simple, but it can't be done by the user in Slide Show View without a button and procedure.

The `AddWorkTogetherSlide` procedure is the real workhorse. It creates a slide like that shown in Figure 10.5.

**Ada is interested in
working with you.**

• Email: ada@loyola.edu

• An idea to ponder: I want to
create a project about butterfiles.

Figure 10.5. Example of Slide Created When Someone Has Chosen to Work with You

This slide will be inserted as the eleventh slide. The following line creates the new slide:

```
ActivePresentation.Slides.Add index:=11, Layout:=ppLayoutText
```

The `index:=11` ensures that the new slide will always be the eleventh slide in the presentation. The `Layout:=ppLayoutText` makes it a standard text slide with a title and one text area. Note that in earlier chapters parameters for procedures and built-in functions were always contained in parentheses. As a general rule, VBA expects something to be returned when the parameters are in parentheses and nothing to be returned when they are not. `ActivePresentation.Slides.Add` could return the slide object that it creates (and we could store that in a variable), but because we left off the parentheses it does not.

Next, we want to add the appropriate text to the slide: the user's name in the title area with a brief message; the user's e-mail address in the text box; and the user's idea (if any) in the text box. The code that adds this follows.

```
With ActivePresentation.Slides(11)
    .Shapes(1).TextFrame.TextRange.Text = userName & _
        " is interested in working with you."
    .Shapes(2).TextFrame.TextRange.Text = "Email: " & userEmail
    With .Shapes(2).TextFrame.TextRange
        If userIdea = "" Then .Text = .Text & Chr$(13) & _
            "No ideas entered" _
            Else .Text = .Text & Chr$(13) & "An idea to ponder: " & userIdea
    End With
End With
```

This uses a couple of `With` blocks (see Chapter 6) and some fairly simple text ideas (see also Chapter 6). The `.Shapes(1)` line sets the text in the title area of the slide. The `.Shapes(2)` line puts the email address in the text area of the slide. Then, the `With` block (through `End With`) adds the user's idea to the text area, or, if the user has no idea, it adds the text "No ideas entered." It's simpler than it looks.

Finally, the `AddNextSlideButton` procedure is called to add a button to go to the next slide:

```
AddNextSlideButton (11)
```

The `AddNextSlideButton` procedure creates a button on any slide. We call it with 11 so it will create a button on the eleventh slide and `index` will be set to whatever number you call `AddNextSlideButton` with (see "Parameters" in Chapter 8 for more information about parameters).

```
Sub AddNextSlideButton(index As Long)
    Dim myShape As Shape
    Set myShape = ActivePresentation.Slides(index).Shapes. _
        AddShape(msoShapeActionButtonForwardorNext, _
        612#, 456#, 82.12, 82.12)
    With myShape.ActionSettings(ppMouseClick)
        .Action = ppActionNextSlide
        .SoundEffect.Type = ppSoundNone
        .AnimateAction = msoTrue
    End With
    With myShape
        .Fill.ForeColor.SchemeColor = ppAccent1
        .Fill.Visible = msoTrue
        .Fill.Solid
        .Line.ForeColor.RGB = RGB(255, 255, 255)
        .Line.Visible = msoTrue
    End With
End Sub
```

In this procedure, the `Set` line creates the button and sets `myShape` to point to it. `msoShapeActionButtonForwardorNext` creates it as a button with a forward-pointing arrow. The first `With` block sets the action (this is what makes it go to the next slide) with the line `.Action = ppActionNextSlide`. The other lines in the first `With` block aren't really necessary but complete the action features of the button.

The second `With` block sets colors (specifically `Fill` and `Line` colors). If you are using the default color scheme, this entire `With` block is unnecessary, but you can play with the parameters to see how the buttons that are created change.

The last thing you should note about this procedure is that it was created using a macro. You can do some things by creating macros by going to the Tools menu and choosing "Record Macro." Whatever you do will be placed into a VBA procedure. This is very good for setting up parameters, such as colors and shapes and locations. However, a macro created in Edit View will not run properly in Slide Show View. Therefore, use the macro to guide you in creating shapes and picking colors, but put those parameters into your own code that will run in Slide Show View. This requires understanding some complicated concepts, so don't worry if you don't get it right away.

Conclusion

In this chapter, you have learned the power of templates. Sometimes you want your students to work on technical skills, but technology in the classroom primarily is a tool for learning the curriculum. As a teacher, you need to balance the use of technology with the needs of the curriculum. If the technology demands are too great, the curriculum will be lost. Templates are the perfect solution for many tasks. If you want your students to use powerful technological features, such as the VBA features of PowerPoint, but you don't want them to focus on the technology, you can create a template with all the features they need, so they can focus on the curriculum but still get the advantage of the powerful features.

You can use templates with your students with early projects while they are still getting used to PowerPoint, or you can use templates for all projects. Templates do not need to include advanced features like VBA. Even the simplest templates (like the Animal Project in Figure 10.1, page 174) can be used to focus your students and limit the amount of technology and design they have to understand.

Exercises to Try

✎ Create a simple presentation (possibly something like the Animal Project shown in Figure 10.1). Save it as a Design Template. Quit PowerPoint and double-click on your template. Observe what happens when you try to save the presentation that is opened.

✎ Pick one of the projects from earlier chapters in this book (the quizzes in Chapter 8 work well as templates) and create a template for your students. Set it up to include all the VBA that is needed, all the basic slides that are needed, and instructions for your students so they know what to do with the project. For example, if you choose a quiz format, you can create the title slide, one question slide, and the feedback slide while giving instructions for how to add new slides and tie the right and wrong answers to the procedures that you have already included.

Epilogue

We have concluded our journey through the scripting features of PowerPoint. But I hope this journey has been only a beginning for you. The book has focused on technical features of PowerPoint, but along the way you have learned some interesting ways to apply the technology with your students because that is the most important thing. You might find it fun to sit around and play with the technical features of PowerPoint, but the bottom line is how it will improve your teaching and your students' learning.

Start small. Create some simple presentations for your students. Don't try to conquer PowerPoint and VBA all at once. A few interactive quizzes won't revolutionize your classroom, but it is a beginning. As you conquer more and more of the examples in this book, you might be ready to create your own examples, or you might want to find more examples. Check out the Web site that accompanies this book at http://www.lu.com. It contains more examples from the author and the opportunity for you to post your own examples and find examples that other readers have posted.

This book was written for scripters. You should be able to copy examples directly from the book and make minor modifications to insert your own content. Many of you will be satisfied to remain a scripter. Just using what is in the book and on the Web site should provide you with a rich set of examples that you can apply to many situations. However, some of you will want more. You will want to create things unlike anything in this book. You will want to become programmers. While there currently are no books geared to educational uses of PowerPoint and VBA, you might be ready for a book that focuses on VBA. Look in the References section for McFedries (1999) or Boctor (1999) or, better yet, go to your local bookstore and browse through a few books. Learning to program is a very personal experience, and a book that one person likes won't make any sense to another. Find one with the right balance of explanations and examples and details that work for you.

As an educator, your focus has to be on the learning of your students. The most important next step is to expand how you can apply multimedia in your classroom. You can do this by creating more and more sophisticated presentations for your students or by expanding your students' role in multimedia production. Chapters 1 and 10 introduced this topic briefly, and you can find more information in Ivers and Barron (2002) and Agnew, Kellerman, and Meyer (1996). If you want to make media production a focal point of your classroom, you might want to check out Counts (2004). If your focus is more on your own media production in a school setting or outside of the schools, you might be interested in Alessi and Trollip (2001), which will take you in the direction of becoming a professional multimedia designer.

Using multimedia that you create and having your students create multimedia can have a powerful impact on the curriculum, and it can help students understand media and gain a level of media literacy. For more information about media literacy, look for the Alliance for a Media Literate America at http://www.nmec.org/.

Your journey is just beginning. You have the power to improve your students' learning. You have the power to use PowerPoint to engage and interact with your students. Technology is not always easy to use, but if you have come this far, you have mastered another piece of powerful technology to help your students learn. Don't stop here. Create exciting interactive presentations. Have your students create exciting interactive presentations. Share your successes, get help with your frustrations, and keep in touch at our Web site, www.lu.com.

References

Agnew, P. W., Kellerman, A. S., & Meyer, J. M. (1996). *Multimedia in the classroom.* Boston: Allyn and Bacon.

Alessi, S. M. & Trollip, S. R. (2001). *Multimedia for learning: Methods and development* (3rd ed.). Boston: Allyn and Bacon.

Alliance for a Media Literate America. (n.d.). Available: http://www.nmec.org/ (accessed January 26, 2004).

Boctor, D. (1999). *Microsoft Office 2000 Visual Basic for Applications fundamentals.* Redmond, WA: Microsoft Press.

Counts, E. L., Jr. (2004). *Multimedia design and production for students and teachers.* Boston: Pearson Education.

Educational Multimedia Fair Use Guidelines Development Committee (1996, July 17). *Fair use guidelines for educational multimedia.* Available: http://www.utsystem.edu/ogc/intellectualproperty/ccmcguid.htm (accessed January 26, 2004).

Goldberg, R. (1996). *The multimedia producers bible.* Chicago: IDG Books Worldwide.

International Society for Technology in Education. (2001). *Educational Computing and Technology Standards for Technology Facilitation Initial Endorsement.* Available: http://cnets.iste.org/ncate/n_fac-stands.html (accessed January 26, 2004).

Ivers, K. S. & Barron, A. E. (2002). *Multimedia projects in education: Designing, producing, and assessing* (2nd ed.). Westport, CT: Libraries Unlimited.

Lehrer, R., Erickson, J., & Connell, T. (1994). Learning by designing hypermedia documents. *Computers in the Schools 10*(1), 227–254.

Liu, M. & Hsiao, Y. (2001). Middle school students as multimedia designers: A project-based learning approach. Paper presented at the National Educational Computing Conference, Chicago, July 25-27, 2001.

Liu, M. & Rutledge, K. (1997). The effect of a "learner as multimedia designer" environment on at-risk high school students' motivation and learning of design knowledge. *Journal of Educational Computing 16*(2), 145–177.

Male, M. (2003). *Technology for inclusion: Meeting the special needs of all students* (4th ed.). Boston: Allyn and Bacon.

McFedries, P. (1999). *VBA for Microsoft Office 2000 unleashed.* Indianapolis, IN: Sams Publishing.

O'Connor, R. J. (1991). Facilitating CAI development via an authoring template. *Computers in the Schools 8*(1/2/3), 249–250.

Pics4Learning copyright-friendly images for education. (n.d.) Available: http://www.pics4learning.com/ (accessed January 26, 2004).

Rindsberg, S. (2003). *PowerPoint FAQ.* Available: http://www.rdpslides.com/ pptfaq/ (accessed January 26, 2004).

Robinette, M. (1995). *Mac multimedia for the teacher.* Braintree, MA: IDG Books Worldwide.

Smithsonian National Museum of American History. (n.d.). *First computer bug.* Available: http://americanhistory.si.edu/csr/comphist/objects/bug.htm (accessed January 26, 2004).

Index

About the Author

DAVID M. MARCOVITZ is Assistant Professor in the Education Department and Coordinator of Graduate Programs in Educational Technology. He received his Ph.D. in Educational Technology from the University of Illinois, Urbana-Champaign, where he studied support for technology in elementary schools. He's taught computer applications and computer programming at the high school level, and he has worked as a technology specialist in a high school. Prior to teaching at Loyola College, he taught in the Educational Technology Program at Florida Atlantic University. He was hired by Loyola College in 1997 to develop a Masters program in Educational Technology, a program he coordinates and for which he teaches many of the classes, including Multimedia Design in the Classroom. He is the author of several articles about educational technology.